# Profile in the Shadows

## Book Two of the Homeless Man's Killer series

A Novel by Karen Roberts

The contents of this work are true events. Some names have been changed by request. The details in this novel and other novels in the Homeless Man's Killer series assisted United States and Canadian authorities in identifying the murders. A special shout-out and praise goes to Natura Pest Control for keeping accurate records. At the time of the first publication, there were eight murder convictions completed. At the time of second publication, there are 185 murder convictions completed in the United States and murder trails are underway in Canada. The murder trials are not complete. The count will increase. Currently the Homeless Man's Killer is the most prolific serial killer in North America and second internationally. When all murder trials are complete, the final count will be a close call with The Beast.

The Whiffle Ball Killer: The Cold Case Murder of Amina Agisheff (Book One of the series)
Profile in the Shadows: Book Two of the Homeless Man's Killer series
His Brunette Alibi: Book Three of the Homeless Man's Killer series

All Rights Reserved

Copyright © 2024 by Karen Roberts. Printing 2024, 2025.

No part of this book may be reproduced or transmitted, downloaded, distributed, reverse engineered, or stored in or introduced into any information storage and retrieval system, in any form or by any means, including photocopying and recording, whether electronic or mechanical, now known or hereinafter invented without permission in writing from KK Roberts Books US.

KK Roberts Books US
PO Box 363
Ridgefield, WA 98642
Visit my website: kkrobertsbooks.us

**ISBN:**
**Hardback:**   979-8-9912353-1-0
**Paperback:**  979-8-9912353-2-7
**eBook:**      979-8-9886431-7-3

# Table of Contents

**They Can Sense Danger**     1

**With This Pen**     7

**The Murder of Jerry Taylor**     11

    **Jerry's Jokes**
    **Housemate**
    **If I Lived in Svaneti**
    **Into the Heated Pool**
    **2009**
    **The Red Padded Jacket**
    **2010**
    **Going Under the Knife**
    **The Last Invite**
    **Wrapped in Mosquito Netting**
    **December 31, 2020**
    **The Red Bag**

**The Padded Jacket**     101

## Blow Up Dolls                                    109

    **Searching the Closets for Blow Up Dolls**
    **Friendly Advice About Cabbage**
    **Nectarine Daquiri**

## The Man Who Left to Buy Groceries     127

## Hair Red Like a Flame                   135

## Kenneth Howard                          139

## Lawrence Otto Olsen                181

    **Otto Spelled Backwards**
    **Skeleton is Found**
    **The Lieutenant**
    **Accepting the Mission**
    **Wolf in Sheep's Clothing**
    **The Red Bag**
    **Tests and Enemies**
    **April 11, 2024**
    **The Approach**
    **Swatting Incident in 2017**
    **Early January 2021**
    **The Ordeal**
    **The Wolf Unclothed**

## The Capture                                    233

# They Can Sense Danger

It was June 1984. We went to a wildlife safari in British Columbia, Canada. I admired the black panther, who is a black spotted leopard. He was so pretty with a glossy black coat. His eyes were blue in the center with yellow around the rim. The eye colors were a beautiful contrast to the black fur. I looked closely, and I could see his black spots in the black fur. Yes, he was a leopard.

The black-spotted leopard looked straight towards me. His pupils dilated. His eyes turned black to match his fur. He took an angry dive. He started to pace along the chain link fence of his cage. He walked back and forth the full length, abruptly turning at each corner. The zookeeper said, "If there was an exit in the chain link fence, he planned to find it or create his own." I wondered if they were feeding the poor cat. I stood still and leaned towards him, trying to assure him I wasn't a threat, trying to understand his reaction. The zookeeper yelled, "Get out of here." I reluctantly walked away towards the next exhibit. The zookeeper mounted the chain link over a building inside the cage and tried to restrain the angry cat.

The leopard didn't calm down. He looked back and up at the zookeeper and then determinedly looked forward. He dived at the front of the cage. He expected the zookeeper to release him. He thought the zookeeper came to be a partner in his escape.

"You think it's her?" another zookeeper asked. He came to assist and viewed the situation, "I think it's him." He pointed to a tall placid man three exhibits away.

The tall man turned his head towards the zookeepers and watched with a non-plussed expression while the two zookeepers partnered in restraining the cat.

I walked on and looked at the hippopotamus. The hippopotamus leaned over and opened his mouth wide for a mouthful of fresh grass. He showed off a large row of teeth and tongue mostly covered in dark green pre-chewed plants. Later the zookeeper approached me, "You need to leave," he said kindly. "It isn't you, it's him." I nodded. He explained, "He is stalking you and it is riling the animals." The zookeeper wasn't talking about the hippopotamus. I tried to drink this in. The zookeeper referred to the quiet man who appeared to stay three exhibits away from me.

The zookeepers continued their conversation a distance away, "He's dangerous and the animals can sense it," the second zookeeper said.

"Shit yeah," answered the first zookeeper who tried to calm the agitated black spotted leopard. "We'll have the authorities take care of him."

I went to the dirt parking lot, into the driver's seat of my car, and waited. My head was down in disappointment. This hadn't gone as I had planned. I rested my forehead on the steering wheel. I wasn't sure what to do. The quiet man a few exhibits away intently watched me. He walked over to my passenger-side door, opened it, and climbed in. I started up the car and drove away.

The zookeepers were shocked into silence. "Well, we knew he was here with someone," one of the zookeepers said. The comment was meant to jolt them out of shock. They turned to stare at each other.

I drove on to the U.S. Canadian border. We switched drivers there. And then switched back again. I drove to a remote camping location and parked in the lot. This was hike in camping. The outing was selected by my companion. "Do I need a parking pass?" I asked.

"No," he said. "It will be fine." We packed gear on our backs, tent, sleeping bags, and necessities. We walked over red rocky hills. The rocks were twelve to eighteen inches across and slid under my feet. Twice I had to steady myself with my right hand and stop to rest. We hiked through a narrow path and green ferns. The floor below us was soft with pine needles. It had more cushion than a track made of recycled rubber tires. It was comfortable for my feet and a pleasant contrast to the red rocks. The air smelled of green plants and distant berries, not huckleberries, something woodsy like salmon berries. Insects buzzed past but did not bite or become a nuisance. The forest was thick there and there was no place to pitch a tent. We walked on to see light gray rocks. We crossed over the rocks to a flat place to pitch a tent near a dry riverbed.

My camping companion looked around the corner and through the trees. "There is another group of campers through there," he said. A short chuckle escaped from his mouth.

"Do you want to go to a different location?" I asked.

"No," he answered. "This is fine."

The tent was pitched over round gray rocks. We didn't bother to stake the tent. We set up our sleeping bags. The small amount of food we packed in was secured inside the tent. "Save it for morning," he said.

It was the longest sunlight day of the year. When the air turned cool with a gentle breeze and the night sky turned dark gray, we retired into the tent. I laid in my sleeping bag. Chipmunks scampered up and down the sides of the tent. They smelled the food and tried to find the entrance. The food they wanted was the graham crackers I bought to make smores. We didn't make a fire, so roasting marshmallows was skipped.

My camping companion rolled over restlessly and then got up to leave the tent. He tapped the side of the tent twice, which scattered the chipmunks. He zipped the tent door open to leave and then zipped the tent door closed. I heard his first three steps on the gray rocks. Then there was silence.

The wind pressed against the sides of the tent, and I began to feel chilled. The tent rain flap grabbed gusts of wind and coughed them back again, filling and collapsing in rhythm. I gave up waiting for my companion and forced myself to sleep. I rolled onto my side. The gray rocks shifted under my weight. I saw him return to the tent in the light of early dawn. He was gone for six hours. I record the time when people start to annoy me.

"Did the chipmunks keep you awake?" I asked him in the morning.

"They were squirrels," he corrected. "And, no, actually I thought they were cute." He smiled.

There wasn't much food to prepare for breakfast and no water source. "Let's break camp," he said. He prepared the gear for transport while I got breakfast ready. I turned around and was startled to see the tent and sleeping bags rolled up and secured onto his backpack.

We munched on breakfast as we hiked out. Before we reached the red rock hill, I heard a loud roar. "What was that?" I asked. I looked back towards the forest.

"Something angry," he said.

"A bear?" I asked. He seemed to nod.

"Keep looking and moving forward. Don't run, walk quickly, and don't stumble" he commanded.

I'd never felt so frightened. I might blame him for riling another animal, but the sound was more than a half mile away. When we reached the red rocks, two hikers started their journey on the trail, a young man and a woman. "A bear," I told them. They smiled. "An angry bear," I clarified. They continued forward.

"Just keep walking forward," the instructions came from behind me. The other couple walked past. When we reached the parking lot, he said, "We made it."

I turned to look at him, expecting him to be looking over his shoulder, worried. Instead, he was standing tall and had a strange smile on his face.

At this hour there were only about five cars in the parking lot. My light blue Nova was about ten parking spaces down.

"That's them," the couple we passed earlier said to the ranger. The young woman was pointing at us.

"I'll let you drive," my camping companion said. I stepped into the driver's seat and started to roll down the window. "Keep your window up," he said. I put my keys in the ignition and placed the car in reverse.

"He had her drive," the ranger pondered with a frown. "Why did he have the nervous one drive?" Something about this scene seemed off.

"I just wanted to know what they saw," the ranger explained.

"She said it was a bear," the female hiker said.

"That wasn't done by a bear," the ranger said.

My companion curled up in the passenger seat and immediately fell asleep. I drove south through Everett and on to Seattle. I looked for a place to stop. "Don't stop at a hotel. They will ask us where we came from," he said.

What a weird thing for him to say. "We came from Kent," I responded.

"Oh, right," he said, "We came from Kent." He smiled contently.

I stopped in Tukwila, and he drove on from there. The next evening, I made smores in the microwave, but he dashed off.

When we visited my parents, he told them I didn't see a bear. I explained, "We heard a bear. I heard a bear."

He said there was no ranger, only other campers. He told them we only went camping once. He gave my parents the impression I was crazy. That is when the defamation started. Already he was planning something.

"You're trying to figure out what he is doing," a dinner guest observed.

"I made the itinerary," I answered. "I know where we went."

# With This Pen

I attended a seminar on How to Write About Trauma without Re-traumatizing Yourself over Zoom. The laptop I used for the seminar is broken at the hinge. "Remember when you came home and wondered what happened to your computer?" my oldest daughter reminded me. The killer snuck into my house and crushed my laptop with his foot. Chunks of plastic broke off the top, but I continue to use the laptop. The media card is failing. There are sound gaps when I play music. The monitor shows green and black static from time to time and won't clear without a computer reboot.

There is a file marked "Public" that I can't access on my computer, and it seems to have forgotten who the Administrator is.

Even the silver and white clip-top pen I use to write this book has a story to tell. It isn't my pen. CM noticed it was out of place. It didn't match the other pens. "All pens are BIC or Pilot brands," she observed.

"Maybe it was Bill's," I suggested to CM. Bill was her father.

"No, I already asked him," CM replied. She talked on the phone with Bill once a week.

I didn't recognize the pen at first. When I first saw it here in my house on the dining room bookshelf, I thought, "Maybe it belongs to the HP pocketbook. It was the same length. But the HP pen was blue. This one was white."

In the dining room, I found BIC pens missing their ink cartridge. I couldn't figure out why. I saw this before. Too long ago, back in 1984. Someone I never thought I'd see again. He took ink cartridges from BIC pens to fill ... I paused in realization ... this pen. I've cleaned out my pen holder many times since then.

Paralyzing fear started to creep in. A scream started to form in the back of my throat but didn't escape. I learned long ago that certain sounds trigger violence. My eyes moved up and to the right to see a memory. The scream in my throat was trapped, just as I felt.

*[I refrain myself from saying, "He was in my house." Waves of nausea keep running over me. I appear without emotion.]*

He received the pen as a gift for being a groomsman when his friend Jim married Marcia. His parents insisted on keeping the pen as compensation for paying for his tuxedo. When his parents moved away, they gave the pen back to him. He was so delighted; he gave the pen a hug to the right side of his face, closed his eyes up tight, and pulled his knees up towards the pen for an extra squeeze. This made his mother laugh. "Other pens are too long and fall out of the pocket," he explained. "This pen is short and just the right size to fit into my shirt pocket," he said with delight. He tucked the pen into his shirt pocket to demonstrate.

Once a classmate at Seattle Pacific University asked to borrow his pen. The classmate clicked the pen closed after use, he held the pen towards his face, studied it for a moment, and then started to walk away with it.

He chased the classmate past the dorm entryway, past the staircase, and down the dormitory hall, and then nearly killed the classmate for not returning it. "It's just a pen," the classmate protested loudly. "What difference does it make if I return it?"

The classmate who returned the pen rounded on me and said, "You are just as bad." He asked, "Why are you defending him?"

"I'm never lending that pen out again," the owner of the pen pouted. "I thought I was going to have to…" His voice trailed off and he had a tone of regret. The sentence was left unfinished. It wasn't necessary. I knew what he was about to say.

# The Murder of Jerry Taylor

## Jerry's Jokes

First, I need to introduce Jerry Taylor. Jerry was born on May 8, 1941. If he was alive, he would be 84 years old. Jerry had light blue eyes. Cheyenne, Wyoming was his hometown. He attended Central High School, class of 1958. Then Jerry graduated from Laramie County Community College, class of 1970. He was a man with a unique sense of humor. He drove a white truck with purple stripes down the side. I assumed he might want the purple stripes removed, but he answered, "Oh no, I want it that way." Jerry Taylor enjoyed standing out from the crowd.

Jerry was in a near-fatal accident while driving his truck. He lost his driver's license and his left arm. But he kept his sense of humor. At this point in life, his hair was white. He had a rounded belly. One time we went to the county fair. I parked on the west side of the fair and Jerry paid for the parking. We rode a buggy shuttle to the yellow gate. Jerry said, "We should try riding the MAX."

Jerry explained, "It is better now that we have more normal folk riding the MAX, businessmen and businesswomen going to work."

He looked at me with a pout, "It used to just be window lickers."

"Window lickers?" I asked. I'm not always aware of new jargon. I wasn't sure if I dared to ask. But for curiosity, I had to ask, "What are window lickers?"

"You know, people sticking out their tongue and licking the window," Jerry explained. He turned his head and stretched out his tongue to the side like a cow reaching for a salt lick by the barn door.

"Oh," I said. "People who need sensory stimulation."

I stopped to consider, "Do they clean the windows?" I'm starting to worry about germs. How safe it is to lick windows? Or sit next to windows someone licked?

"Sometimes," Jerry answered with a chuckle.

I sighed, "We could ride the MAX next time." There probably wouldn't be too many window lickers and maybe the window would be cleaned.

We stepped off the buggy and went in through the yellow gate. Jerry stopped to look at the antique machinery. I stood at his side and watched him. He bent over to take a closer look and then looked back at me and smiled. These were his favorite exhibits. We went past the horse barn and cow barns. We vowed to return for ice cream later in the day. We stepped into the main exhibit hall to escape the heat of the sun.

We were looking at the quilt exhibit. He let me lead him there. He was courteous to browse exhibits of my interests. An elderly woman was sitting at the table, handing out pencils, and collecting votes for "Best Quilt, People's Choice". Her grayish-white curls looked soft and full. She turned to chat with a younger woman sitting next to her. Jerry looked at the volunteer and joked about the quilt hanging on the wall. "That is so beautiful," Jerry said. "I'd give my left arm for it," and then he moved his stump where his left arm would have been.

The volunteer turned her head, looked up at Jerry in alarm, and then burst out into laughter. "Oh, my word," she gasped. She put her hand up to her mouth. If she was wearing false teeth, the gesture held them in place. She appreciated his humor.

"When I say that, the person either laughs or screams," he chuckled. "Men or women," Jerry looked at me and bragged with a chuckle. "I love messing with people," he said with laugh lines that spread across his cheeks and a sparkle in his blue eyes. He was in his sixties then and had balding white hair. He kept himself clean and showered. Cleanliness was a practice his mother instilled in him. "I always thank my mother for that," he praised. "My good eyesight is another gift from my mother."

"I wish I had the gift of good eyesight," I said. He led me to his choice, which was the main exhibit. It was a large sand sculpture. By large, I mean it was huge. It was an island with hills, a sandcastle, and monstrous-sized lizards all made of sand. We gasped in amazement.

I drove Jerry home. The air conditioning helped cool us down after the hot day at the fair. He turned down the volume on my car radio several turns. It was his way of saying he wanted to chat. He pointed to the white-painted structure where he lived. I pulled over to the side of the road to let him out of my car.

Jerry lived in a small room at 111 ½ Fourth Avenue, the east half of the half. He had instructions to keep his interior bedroom door closed. The west half of the half was rented to another family. This apartment was so small you might walk past it repeatedly and never notice it was there. The white building was tucked behind the main house. The apartment only had an outside door and a bathroom. Jerry had a large television set that he kept on for background noise. He didn't have a bed frame, so he piled a queen-sized mattress on top of an old hide-a-bed. He didn't have room for both.

His front lawn was the backyard of the main house. The lawn was a large patch of grass and dandelions and in need of a mow when he moved in. "Can I mow the lawn for you?" Jerry asked his neighbors.

They nodded with big smiles and happily agreed. "Woo Hoo!" Jerry said, "Then it's a deal." There were dandelions and weeds, but he cleaned that up.

There was no kitchen. The kitchen belonged to the west half of the half. "I rarely cook," Jerry said. "Besides, I don't need it with the deli right next door," he chuckled. He referred to the Starliner. He was on a first-name basis with the deli owner. The deli sold sandwiches, groceries, and the local newspaper. The deli was to the right of his apartment. The firehouse was to the rear.

Jerry worked security at night. He was also a semi-retired welder. Jerry continued to work as a welder after losing his arm. He had strong supports that hung together like a monkey chain. These supports were made of thick black plastic and reinforced in the center with four screws spaced in the shape of a square, rotated to an equal-sided rhombus. The support chain held the metal item in place while he worked with the welding equipment with his right arm. "I'll never part with these. I can't do my work without them," he said solemnly. "You can't buy them anywhere." Essentially the support chain was his left arm.

Jerry welded wheelbarrows and carts. One of his carts was on display on the old main road out of town. Recently he accepted and finished a welding job at a local wedding venue. The wedding venue was a white two-story building that used to be a church. Jerry's wrought iron pieces twisted into symmetrical shapes and became decorations in the courtyard. The courtyard extended to the south of the building and provided an entrance for the caterers. Just beyond that was a small park that overlooked the river below.

Historically the river was a mode of transportation. Before roads were built, boats proudly transported goods into the area and freight trains continued the voyage. Lumberjacks stood on logs and used oars to route the timber down the slough and into the port. The river flowed south as high tide receded and north after low tide. The tide and the blowing wind allowed them to go up and down the river without a motor. Now with improved roads, the river was no longer a passage for goods. The freight trains and passenger trains no longer stopped. The only boats were for recreation or fishing. The marina gave the area a beach-town presence.

# Housemate

Some of the names are changed.

Jerry wanted a place that would allow space for his welding. He was looking for a place with a garage, but he needed to be close to the bus stop. Hephzibah was looking for a place to live. She had accepted a job nearby. Jerry thought they might team up. Hephzibah suggested a house for rent on Main. Jerry gave it a look over, but he decided against it. "I looked at the place. There is no garage, only a carport." He explained, "I need a garage to do my welding."

"There is a carport off to the side," Hephzibah explained. "But there is a garage that is no longer used in the front of the house to the left of the kitchen." Before Jerry had an opportunity to take a second look, the property was sold to an investor. "It was bought as an investment property," Hephzibah responded. The new owners liked how close it was to town and thought it might become industrial property one day.

They needed to be quicker. Afterward, Jerry took another look at the house. This time he noticed the garage. "I finally saw the garage at the house you were talking about," Jerry said to Hephzibah. "It would have been perfect," Jerry admitted. "Next time," he said regretfully.

The next rental that became available was also on Main. It was a two-story centennial house with a shed in the back. Hephzibah thought the shed might be a place for his welding. Jerry said, "I'm not certain about using the shed for welding. I need a sturdy roof to hang things on." However, he accepted the offer to move in.

Two muscular firemen moved Jerry's hide-a-bed and other items, including the large television set. They completed the errand in a couple of hours. The heavy hide-a-bed remained on the main floor in the living room as a sofa. Even though Jerry and Hephzibah combined their belongings, the large living room quickly swallowed the small amount of furniture. The living room had a natural gas stove for heat and twelve-foot vaulted ceilings. The staircase had a ninety-degree turn and was supported from below with a solid wood railing five inches thick. All bedrooms were upstairs. Hephzibah had a spare bed that she placed in the largest bedroom for Jerry to use. Tabitha and Rachel moved into the smaller bedrooms.

Tabitha and Rachel were placed in Hephzibah's care by the court. Hephzibah provided for them financially. The situation was both a blessing and a challenge. Sometimes it was overwhelming, but they weren't mischievous. They were amazing girls.

Hephzibah showed Jerry around the house. She went into the kitchen, faced him, and gestured to the left. She proudly told Jerry, "And it has a dishwasher!"

Jerry answered, "But we won't run the dishwasher." He looked straight at Hephzibah's face and said in a definite tone, "We'll just wash the dishes by hand to save on utilities."

"Are you volunteering to handwash dishes?" Hephzibah hesitantly asked. She interpreted his comment as a suggestion.

"It does save," Jerry paused for emphasis, "On both electricity and water." He smiled and then gave a serious glance, with a mild look of shock at Hephzibah's non-compliance with his request. She had too much on her plate to work full-time and do extra cleaning. This was the start of a series of mild disagreements.

Jerry called the landlord and asked him for a new shower head. The landlord was standing in Hephzibah's bathroom, leaning over the tub shower when she came home from work. "A man with one arm can't hold the shower and bathe at the same time," Jerry said. He looked at her with a smile that showed the wrinkles at the corners of his eyes.

The situation was embarrassing for Hephzibah who liked the flexible shower head and didn't want to bother the landlord for a replacement. She took the dangling shower head and fastened it on the holder. It wasn't an argument with Jerry, but it was another subtle disagreement. Jerry looked from her to the shower head and left it at that.

Another disagreement was when Jerry called the landlord to fix the toilet because the back of the toilet was "leaking." The toilet wasn't leaking, it was plugged up. This time the plumber came to repair. The plumber stood near the toilet and explained the issue to Hephzibah. The landlord called Hephzibah to ensure the repair was done. Jerry's requests from the landlord were embarrassing to Hephzibah who preferred to fix things herself and not be troublesome.

On the night shift, Jerry was a security officer at a local Seventh Day Adventist church. This was a new building under construction and located along the freeway. The church administrators let him stay out in the trailer when he was there. He was allowed to take naps in the trailer during his shift. He made his rounds and patrolled the buildings. "They added stocking the toilet paper to my chores. Woo hoo!" Jerry boasted with a proud smile. "I love having something to do."

In the mornings after his shift, the men from the church went out to coffee at the Country Café. One of the men provided Jerry with a ride back to town. They discussed extending the job contract. Jerry joked, "I can fall asleep on the job just as good as the next guy." However, the church administrators decided to replace him with a man who attended the church. Jerry was confused by the decision and worried they didn't accept his sense of humor.

Jerry only stayed at the house on Main for a couple of months. He had second thoughts about moving in with young women and worried there might be rumors or legal ramifications. He planned to move to the country. But that didn't work out. There wasn't reliable public transportation. Instead, he moved to senior apartments in the city. He left his hide-a-bed, chest of drawers, mirror, and television set behind at Hephzibah's house, along with several other items.

Jerry left his liquid pint measuring cup behind and a large container of black pepper. "Can't you take this container of black pepper with you?" Hephzibah asked. She grasped the pepper with her right hand and extended her arm to hold it out in Jerry's direction.

"You can use it," Jerry decided. He looked back at her with quizzical eyes and a mouth pulled up in the left corner. He planned to take as few items as possible for the next move.

"No, I really can't," Hephzibah explained. Her usual easy-going personality was gone. This container added to her clutter. It was too large to fit on her alphabetized spice shelf. Her spice shelf was made from an old wooden "Beauty Bath Seeds" container hung onto the wall. Jerry didn't take the hint. The black pepper remained with Hephzibah who struggled to find a place for it. Fifteen years passed before she ran out of black pepper.

## If I Lived in Svaneti

Hephzibah had a problem at her job. She worked at a mineral processing plant. Her supervisor arrived at 9:00 a.m. and walked through the control room towards his small office in the back room. The control room had five central processing units CPUs that Hephzibah monitored. The CPUs obtained information from Programmable Logic Controllers PLCs in the field. She said to her supervisor, "I check the trending graphs each morning at the start of my shift. My shift starts at 8:00 a.m. and I'm in the control room checking the graphs at 7:50 a.m." Hephzibah continued, "I check the trending graphs throughout the day. I'm quick to notice issues and correct them. But this wasn't a normal problem. Some mornings there was a flood in the main pump room."

Hephzibah's supervisor checked the trending graphs for spikes, checked the main pump room, and then complained, "This was caused by a PLC that seems to revert from English to Svan, as if by default."

Svan is a language spoken by the Svani, who live in Svaneti. The small region is on the southern border of Russia, east of the Black Sea, and north of Turkey in the country of Georgia. The Svani uses the metric system units of measure. The language change simultaneously altered the units on the flow from British units to metric.

The change from gallons to kiloliters without a change in the values caused the change in the parameters used for control. The pump sped up to meet the new control values. Flooding was the final result. After diagnosing the problem and locating the issue, many mornings, Hephzibah had to go into the main pump room to reset the PLC back to English. The instructions on the PLC screen were in Svan, so she had to memorize each screen and count to know what to select. Once the controller was back in English, the problem was temporarily solved.

Hephzibah made several calls to PLC technical support to find the issue or a fix. There didn't seem to be any software problem that caused the language change. The pressure washer started his shift at 6:00 a.m. and might have sprayed the PLC before 7:00 a.m. But the trend shifted four-and-a-half hours earlier. As a precaution, the pressure washer was told to avoid spraying the PLCs. The problem continued. Often the trend shifted at about 1:30 or 2:00 a.m. This was the time when the night shift was doing their after-lunch stretches in the control room.

Finally, the company determined that the PLC was intentionally sabotaged. There wasn't a security setting to protect the PLC from an unintentional language change. Every solution was tried. "I guess it is because we want people to read it," technical support confessed. "We'll add that to our list of firmware updates." Firmware is in the vague space between hardware and software.

That morning there was another prank. A water valve was left on. Hephzibah waded through a six-inch-deep flood to turn off the hose. Instead of praise for catching the problem, she was asked to leave the control room and come to the lunchroom near the main office. It was furnished with a long rectangular table with many folding chairs, and a water fountain. A small bathroom was on the farthest end. "Do you know of someone who likes to play practical jokes?" the new Human Resources Assistant asked her.

"Yes, I do," Hephzibah admitted. Her response was met with silence. She gestured in the direction of the manufacturing plant. "What kind of things are we talking about?" she asked. There was no response. "More information on the practical jokes might narrow this down," she added. The HR Assistant didn't respond. She asked a reasonable question. She wasn't certain the events at the site were pranks. She preferred to assume positive intent until no other solution was found.

The HR Assistant snapped, "It doesn't matter."

Hephzibah was the one who caught the problems with the pumps or the valves because her Supervisory Control and Data Acquisition SCADA graphs told her where to look. She didn't cause these problems. Her work shift started at 8:00 a.m., six hours after the trend change on the graphs. She could show this on her graphs if she could return to her control room. Right now, she was in the lunchroom with a man from Human Resources with no hope of returning to the evidence to clear her of wrongdoing. She was at home at the time the changes took place and there were witnesses to where she was. The time discrepancy didn't matter to her employer. He theorized she might sneak out of the house, make the changes, and then return home.

The HR Assistant said Hephzibah was "bad for the work-family" and didn't explain why. Everything she was taught to view as immoral was what she was accused of doing.

A man at the coffee shop told her, "Maybe that isn't a coincidence. Someone intentionally accuses you of doing the things that are immoral to you." His clue was well-intentioned but didn't narrow it down.

The PLC technical support provided a firmware re-flash that addressed Hephzibah's concern about the need for security in the language setting. The problems at the manufacturing plant stopped immediately after she left. This didn't point to a problem with her. This pointed to a problem that was traveling with her. Those who worked closest to her missed her expertise in the manufacturing plant.

The looming uncertainty of the situation caused Hephzibah's usual easy-going personality to shift. In a way, she became more aware of the danger. In another way, she became less aware of personal relationships. The actions she did to keep her job were not the correct actions. Her personality needed to shine through. But her personality shifted to someone who was frantically trying to control a situation that was sliding out of control. To top this off, Jerry moved out. This wasn't the best time to lose the financial help of a boarder.

## Into the Heated Pool

The senior apartments Jerry moved into were fully furnished. There was a heated pool next to the main office for guests. Jerry invited Hephzibah over for a swim. She didn't usually go to senior apartments. But she appreciated his invitation and accepted. He kept his thin white short-sleeve undershirt on to hide his stump. The pool was warm, like bathwater. They stayed in the four-foot section, while the children with floatation devices paddled in the shallow end and the serious swimmers stayed in the deep end. A young blonde boy wearing floatation around his waist paddled in our direction and closely watched his mother, who smiled at his progress. "He is so cute," Jerry praised. The boy returned to the sounds of children splashing and laughing in the shallow end.

"There isn't too much chlorine in the pool. Check it out," Jerry said with fascination. "Put your face down in the water and open your eyes." Their eyes didn't sting when opened under the water. However, the pool was clean and free of debris. "They must clean this pool regularly," Jerry praised with a broad smile.

Jerry climbed out of the pool, shook off the water out of his hair, and stepped through the sliding glass doors. He dried off inside next to the fireplace in the main office. Jerry joked to the senior women, "I'm available to offer my services as a gigolo," he said with a large grin. The response from the elderly women was wide horrified eyes, mouths pursed closed, and no laughs. "I never get any takers on that one," Jerry complained, shaking his head.

For reasons I'll never know, Jerry was evicted for breaking the apartment rules. Hephzibah worried he was evicted for asking her to come to the pool. She called the senior apartments to inquire. The only response she received was from the apartment manager. "He knows what he did," was her grave reply.

Jerry was accepted to live at the Highland Park Apartment. This apartment was a better fit, and the room was fully furnished. The seniors shared the same entranceway but were spread out in different sections and on different floors of the building. "You can visit who you want," Jerry explained. Jerry gave the small living room an inviting appeal by turning the blinds a quarter turn and hanging green plants from his black welding supports. From the information I've gathered so far this was Jerry J. Taylor's last known address, Highland Park Apartments.

Later Jerry invited Hephzibah to see an outdoor Concert in the Park at Ester Short Park, in part of the Saturday Market area. The concerts were given each Thursday evening. Ester Short Park was in the middle of downtown. The Saturday Market area was mostly vacant now with only a few food vendors. One vendor sold hot dogs. Another vendor sold pretzels. On Saturday the area would be filled with sweet smells, fresh produce, bundles of lavender, and flower bouquets. Jerry brought lawn chairs to sit on. Most of the attendees were sitting on blankets. No one complained about his lawn chairs, because they saw he was disabled.

Jerry and Hephzibah talked about gardening. Jerry left to buy dinner. He paused to talk with a lady. She encouraged him to buy from the Subway Lite menu. Jerry was late returning with dinner. He came back with a twelve-inch vegetable Subway sandwich with a double portion of mustard. The result was a vegetable and mustard sandwich. He sat down in the lawn chair. Hephzibah held his sandwich while he sat down. Everything is a little harder with only one arm. He offered to share his sandwich.

Hephzibah gasped in irritation, "Vegetables and mustard on a sandwich? Why?"

Jerry looked at her with surprise and alarm, "It was a low-calorie option," he explained.

"Okay," Hephzibah acknowledged.

The musicians performed fifties music. The man playing the guitar had slicked back hair, while the lead singer came on stage wearing a blonde wig and a pink poodle skirt. A poodle skirt is wide at the bottom, made of felt, with an applique of a poodle on a leash along the edge. All the performers wore tap shoes.

Ester Short Park had a farmer's market on the weekend. They went back on Saturday and viewed the artwork and visited the produce stand. Both selected vegetables to bring home. They waited for a street vendor to prepare a special rice dish called gumbo with shrimp and capers.

The cook seemed apprehensive. "The shrimp gumbo will be about an hour and a half," he said. He encouraged the chicken, arroz con pollo. "The chicken is ready now." The arroz con pollo was in a sealed white plastic container. The steel bowl the arroz con pollo was cooked in was cleaned and ready for the next batch. The tarp over the table provided shade for the ingredients, but the shade only extended for a short distance. The eager patrons stood in the bright sunlight.

Hephzibah ordered, "I'll have the chicken, arroz con pollo."

She looked at Jerry, "Are you ordering the same?"

Jerry shook his head and faced towards the cook, "I'll have the shrimp gumbo." Before he paid, he turned towards Hephzibah and asked, "You want it too? Don't you?" He was certain she agreed.

Hephzibah accommodated the cook, "I'm fine. I'll take the chicken." She smiled at the cook. The arroz con pollo was sitting too long, and the rice was becoming mushy. The cook would need to toss it if he couldn't find buyers.

"He doesn't want to cook it," Jerry commented. The shrimp gumbo wasn't ready. It wasn't even started. The ingredients lay separately in containers on the table. The cook stood looking at the crowd. "It's on the menu and it's what I want," Jerry explained. "I'm willing to wait."

"It only stays fresh for so long after it is cooked," Hephzibah explained a possible reason for the delay. The arroz con pollo was starting to stick together. It was pressed in the plastic container waiting for a buyer. While they waited, Hephzibah told Jerry about the garden she planted.

The cook stopped writing numbers on his pad and started up a fire. He placed the steel bowl over the fire and drizzled olive oil. The oil sizzled as he quickly grabbed the other ingredients. The onions were already chopped and waiting to go first. He didn't explain his technique to the audience or the reason for his choices. He quietly went to work. Yet, his performance of cooking over a fire was part of the customer experience.

"He waited until he had a certain number of buyers before he started it," Jerry noted. Jerry was hungry in anticipation. The aroma of sautéed onions filled the tented area. Hephzibah stood back to ensure Jerry had a front-row view as the cook prepared the dish in front of him. The other ingredients were tossed in one by one. The cook stirred with a long-handled metal spoon to mix the flavors and prevent burning. Jerry was pleased with the result.

Earlier that summer, Hephzibah watched the cook on the street in front of the old theater. The smell of rich spices tickled her senses, cumin, paprika, chili powder, red cayenne pepper, onions, garlic, coriander, salt, and pepper. The sound of sizzling food emerged from the steel bowl as he demonstrated his technique. "You need to work fast and have the ingredients ready and at hand," he explained. "It isn't enough to have the jar of capers. The lid needs to be off of the jar and the amount premeasured." He chuckled, "I learned that the hard way." He explained each ingredient as he added it, whether it was part of the original recipe or an addition of his own. This was arroz con pollo. "I learned how by watching a man on the street in New Orleans," the cook explained. It was a fascinating process. He smiled and proudly served to an eager, waiting audience.

The aroma and fragrant steam wafted through the air. People clapped. A man with a small dog on a leash stepped up to accept his dinner from the cook. The dog looked from the cook to his owner and wagged his tail in hope, before accepting the food was not for him. The experience was similar to watching a street musician play the drums. Hephzibah looked at the sidewalk near the cook for an empty violin case to toss in tips. But the price of the food was the only expectation.

Jerry and Hephzibah went to the end of the market and turned the corner to the right. A table offered berries by the half flat. Hephzibah requested from the cashier, "I'll take the blueberry and strawberry half flat." She pointed to a mixture, "That one." The clerk moved to wrap the container.

Hephzibah told Jerry, "I planted a garden at the house. I planted ever-bearing strawberries in front and raspberries in back." She turned towards the clerk to pay. "I planted butter crunch lettuce in a hanging basket and other vegetables in the backyard near the raspberries. I'm waiting to see what comes up."

## 2009

Hephzibah was on her own now, taking care of Tabitha and Rachel. A brown recluse spider found a home in the doorway to their only bathroom. Hephzibah tried to walk out of the bathroom to the kitchen. The brown recluse lowered itself on his retreat web. Hephzibah caught sight of it. She told Rachel to take the fly swatter out of the closet and slide it across the floor. She had no one else available to help. Hephzibah knew she only had one chance at the spider. She caught the spider in mid-air with the fly swatter and slammed it to the ground. She handled the situation beautifully. But she was not done looking over her shoulder. This was the first time Tabitha and Rachel noticed Hephzibah's personality starting to shift, and the shift stayed.

A staffing firm contacted Hephzibah for a new job as an Electrical Engineer. The position was more money than her previous work. She didn't complain. The work was interesting too. She took to it like a duck to water and hit the ground running. The career path also provided an opportunity to work with imaginary numbers, integrals, and derivatives. These were areas where she excelled. The work was a part of Remedial Action Schemes. In layman's terms that is referred to as, "Making sure we don't burn a big hole in the ground."

Hephzibah bought a house in a quiet neighborhood near the kayak launch. She loved the yard, the tulips, and the irises that bloomed in the spring. Her realtor was RE/MAX. The realty agent asked her to shuffle her feet down the hallway. "See how level that is!" the agent exclaimed. It was true. The foundation of the house was solid. This was a bonus and one less thing to worry about.

People from her work, her neighborhood, and her church helped with the move. She planned to serve them lunch. This was an extra challenge because the refrigerator had not been delivered yet. With everyone pitching in to help, the work was completed before lunch. They left for home. The delivery truck arrived with the refrigerator at the old house. They telephoned about their arrival. "You are at the wrong house," Hephzibah explained. "I'll walk over to your truck and tell you where to go."

"Won't that be a long walk?" the delivery men asked. He was on a schedule.

"No, I only moved a block and a half," Hephzibah replied with a small laugh.

"You can just tell us where to go," the truck driver responded.

"I am one block north and one block west," Hephzibah answered.

"That is two blocks," they complained. "You are really making us work." Then they chuckled.

Hephzibah found their truck and pointed to where they needed to go. They moved the refrigerator towards the back of the truck and then let down a hydraulic lift. They placed an instant ramp over the front step and walked the refrigerator in. They plugged in the appliance and left. "That's all we do," they said as they closed the front door behind them. Hephzibah scooted the refrigerator into place. With the refrigerator delivered, the house was now complete.

Hephzibah asked the landlord for permission to dig up the raspberries she planted at the rental house. The landlord agreed. She planted a garden next to the garden shed with plenty of fertilizer, another garden on the west side of the house, and transplanted the raspberries on the south end. The west side garden attracted honeybees.

It was a sunny day in July 2009. Hephzibah enjoyed the local 5K fun run and she kept in shape for upcoming races. The honeybees buzzed around the dandelions, as Hephzibah walked through the path towards the front door of her house. Stray daisies bloomed as decorative weeds. Hephzibah stepped through the front door of her house. The CD player sat on the oak end table near the front door. The Sting album, "The Dream of The Blue Turtles," was lying next to the CD player. The CD player was on. The song "Moon Over Bourbon Street" played with the lyrics, "I must love what I destroy and destroy the thing I love. Oh, you'll never see my face or hear the sound of my feet. While there's a moon over Bourbon Street."

It wasn't like Tabitha to leave electricity on when she left the house. Tabitha was a master at energy conservation and reduction of her ecological footprint. She calculated the best way to mow the lawn and urged others to follow. For a while, they mowed with a simple reel mower, instead of a lawnmower powered with gasoline. When Tabitha came home, Hephzibah complimented Tabitha for expanding her musical genre to include Sting. But Tabitha denied playing the Sting album. "Why would I listen to that?" she asked in an appalled tone. Hephzibah picked up the CD case. She gave it a contemplative look. She looked around the room and didn't see anything missing.

Hephzibah repainted the house with Miller paint in light and dark browns with black trim. She painted the front and back doors red and the garage door dark brown for contrast. The house looked cute. She unpacked all of the boxes except a few. Some items from the move were not yet put away and remained in the garage.

One of the items in the garage was a wicker basket of gently used toys. Rachel noticed something strange. The remote-controlled toy truck was out of the wicker basket in the garage. "Who has been playing with the remote-control car in the garage?" Rachel asked. Later she noticed the truck was in the basket, but in a different place in the basket.

Rachel and Tabitha suspected the three neighbor children first. The neighbor children insisted to Rachel and Tabitha, "We didn't go into that garage." Rachel and Tabitha believed them.

In the garage Hephzibah found a broom with a red handle. She assumed the broom was left by the previous owner. She designated the broom with the red handle for outdoor sweeping. The broom with the yellow handle was designated for indoor sweeping. In this way, the yellow handled broom would not become muddy. Gardening tools, such as the hoe, shovel, and garden rake were placed in the gardening shed.

A river ran through the city; it flowed into a deeper river that served to separate two states. The deeper river, with its strong currents and undertow, carries cargo barges inbound from the ocean. A slough branches off the deeper river; it meets another river that flows off a lake. Together, the deeper river, lake river and slough create an island.

Hephzibah walked down to the marina. She was pleased to find that her house was so close to this attraction. The sun was just starting to set on the horizon. There was plenty of light remaining in the day. The breeze was cool. Two old men stood talking along the path that followed the river.

"A man went that way with a shovel," the taller man said while he kept his eyes on the water. The concerned citizen had brown eyes and mousey brown, peppered hair and wore a tan hat.

"I think he went that way," the shorter man determined. He had blue eyes, light gray hair and a soft weathered face with fine wrinkles. He pointed across the river to the west.

"I expected him to come back up again," the taller man said. He continued a steady eye on the river facing north. He waited for the man to come up for air.

"There is nothing but rocks along the shore," Hephzibah commented. What did the man mean by "come back up again"? Come up from where?

"You'd better lock your shovel up in the garage," the shorter man said. "Other homes in the area need to be on the lookout too."

Hephzibah went home. She looked in the garden shed. She couldn't find her shovel. She looked in the garage. She couldn't find her shovel. She stopped to think of where the shovel might be. There were many houses in between hers and the marina. It would be paranoid to assume the shovel at the marina was hers. When the shovel appeared again, it was in the garage next to the broom with the red handle. Hephzibah rubbed her forehead with her right hand.

The area behind Hephzibah's garage had a motion sensor light. Someone worked hard to break it. First, the light cover was removed. This made the light brighter, instead of dimmer when it came on. The brighter light caused the neighbor's dog to bark. Then the cover for the sensor was smashed in. This final act destroyed the motion sensor and the light.

This intrusion was followed by a bullet hole in Hephzibah's bedroom window. The bullet hole was from a BB gun. It was the height of a child, and it was shot from the direction of the neighbor's house. Hephzibah learned the neighbors cared for three grandchildren while their daughter was doing time for methamphetamine use. At the start of the school year, the oldest boy of the three children was expelled from school for bringing a weapon to class. He was in elementary school. He owned a BB gun. All three children insisted they didn't do it.

There was a new bullet hole, two months after the first. It was the height of a tall adult male. Hephzibah surveyed the scene. There was a fishing boat turned on its side along the neighbor's house. Maybe the neighbor boy stood on the boat and fired his gun at her bedroom window? "The bullet holes in my bedroom window are unsettling," Hephzibah complained to Bill Dole, her mentor at work.

"Contact the local police," Mr. Dole said. He nodded for her to know that was the definite course of action. "The neighbor should pay for the broken window," he advised. "Even if it was a baseball accidentally breaking a neighbor's window, the neighbor would pay." Hephzibah contacted the local police.

The local policeman looked at the height of the fishing boat. He dismissed the idea that someone stood on the boat for the second shot. He said, "I can't make sense of bullet holes from two different shooters." The police noticed the broken motion sensor light and crossed over to the garage door. He noticed the door frame on the garage door was cracked near the lock. "Someone wanted to get in here really bad," he commented. He reached inside the garage door to flip the light switch on and off.

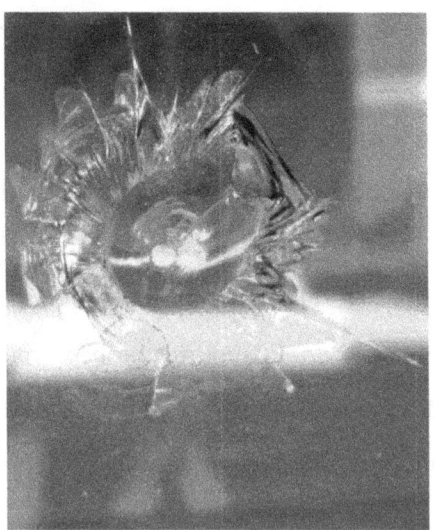

Bullet hole in Hephzibah's bedroom window.

Hephzibah explained to the police officer, "The light was working when I bought the house." The policeman was ready to dismiss it. The police contacted the previous owner who verified the motion sensor light was working. He said it must have been disabled by someone who was living with Hephzibah. However, the previous owner insisted that she was sure Hephzibah lived alone and that no men were living in the house. She didn't count Tabitha and Rachel because they were minors.

Hephzibah wanted her bedroom window replaced to get rid of the bullet holes. She contacted a window replacement company. She hoped for a soundproof window to muffle the noise at night as an upgrade. She could hear the barges blowing their horns as they traveled down the river. The passing trains made a grinding sound on the railroad tracks and blew their whistles. She could hear the neighbor outside as she was trying to sleep.

"I don't think that sound is from my side of the fence," the neighbor said. "I think it is from your side of the fence and from under your house." He pointed down, "I see a light shining through the crack."

"What crack?" Hephzibah wondered. She looked inside and outside. She couldn't find a crack.

The window salesman argued over the effectiveness of soundproof windows and said the new building codes would require the bedroom window to be cut one-half inch wider. Hephzibah reasoned she would replace her bedroom window later, although the lingering bullet holes in her bedroom window did not put her at ease. Instead, she purchased a bay window for the living room and a garden window for the kitchen. She was determined to use the opportunity for an upgrade. This approach increased her optimism.

Hephzibah locked the garden shed door when she first purchased the house. But she stopped closing the lock when it became difficult to find the key. After each use, she replaced the key on the fourth hook of the key holder inside the house near the front door. But she seemed to be misplacing the key. The key wasn't where she remembered placing it. She worried there would be no way to open up the shed door. Most importantly, she needed access to the shed. After that, she left the lock open on the shed door and did not secure it. She checked. Nothing was missing from the shed.

Hephzibah trusted that she lived in a safe neighborhood. There were minor adjustments to the move. But there was an undercurrent happening that she couldn't see. This undercurrent was affecting her position at her workplace.

Work at Remedial Action Schemes became icy. A new work supervisor moved in. There was a rumor that Hephzibah was dishonest. Her work suspected that she didn't buy the house and was just pulling their leg. There was another rumor that she didn't really have a bachelor's degree. The previous supervisor who hired her said, "Your physics degree and graduate work make you more than qualified for the position." She patted her hand on the table as emphasis while closing the deal. The new rumors were carried out behind the scenes. So, Hephzibah had no way to address the allegations. She was escorted to the door by the human resource director without an explanation of why.

All Hephzibah knew was that her hair was falling out. Her doctor could not find the cause. Her bloodwork was normal. Hephzibah's doctor decided she was depressed. The human resource director was fired later, but this did not reconcile Hephzibah's work situation. Hephzibah took a job at Hewlett-Packard.

Tabitha's bedroom was on the southwest corner of the house. Her window screen was replaced with a new one when the house was first purchased. The old window screen was tattered and allowed insects to fly in. Tabitha's new window screen was now bent on the middle right side from someone taking the screen off from the outside. Tabitha was frustrated. She decided the new screen was better than the old screen. "The bottom line is, I need to keep insects from flying into the room."

Their neighbor, Lee's motion sensor light kept turning on at night. The light was shining bright into Tabitha's window. Lee told Tabitha, "I know I have a problem." Lee pondered, "I'm trying to think of what to do." Lee moved the motion sensor light from the house onto his garden shed.

This made the motion sensor light harder to trigger. When that wasn't enough, Lee left the electrical switch off. He laughed at his solution to the problem.

While Hephzibah was at work, the card table moved from the garage to the dining room in Hephzibah's house. The card table was folded up and placed against the wall. It rested against the chains of the weights for the cuckoo clock. This broke the mechanism in the recently repaired clock. In the hallway closet, the board games were tilted. The game of Risk, which was keeping the stack of games straight, moved from near the bottom to the top of the stack. The more rectangular Aggravation game was first balanced across two stacks. With the shift in order, the Aggravation game was closer to the bottom and tilted at an angle. Hephzibah straightened the stack. When she checked the closet later the games were tilted again. The Risk game was back to the top. Tabitha and Rachel insisted they never played Risk.

# The Red Padded Jacket

Hephzibah invited Jerry to Thanksgiving dinner. She wanted him to see her new house. She placed a goose in the oven, covered in foil. The potatoes were peeled and put in a pan of water in the oven next to the goose. Jerry thought it would be a good idea to take in a movie while the goose cooked. "The meal will take a while and this was an opportunity for fun," Jerry explained.

Hephzibah drove everyone across town to the Cascade Theater, or where she thought the theater was. She found the theater had moved to a new location, and she was becoming nervous trying to find the new theater address. They arrived at the theater with only one minute to spare. Jerry thought the theater was easy to access, because he was thinking about accessing from the bus line, his usual mode of transportation now.

After the movie, Hephzibah was worried about leaving the house with the oven on. This was her first attempt at cooking a goose and she wasn't sure how it would turn out. She expected to return home to a burnt goose or possibly dry meat. To her surprise, the timing was just right. The goose was perfect. Jerry worried about the potatoes. Those were perfect too. The meal was very good. After dinner, she put some leftover goose meat into a Tupperware bowl with a blue lid for Jerry to take home.

The events of the holiday went well until Hephzibah tried to return some of Jerry's things. She knew he couldn't take back the hide-a-bed, because he didn't have room for it, and it would be impossible to haul up the winding stairs to his apartment. He didn't need his television set, dresser, or mirror, because his furnished apartment already had those. She explained, "I donated your television set to charity." Jerry accepted her decision. The dresser and mirror were in Rachel's bedroom. Jerry sat down on the sofa to watch the Macy's Thanksgiving Day Parade on her television.

Hephzibah brought out the other items for Jerry to take home. She found a blue bath towel she accidentally bleached in the warm water wash, a man's red and black plaid insulated coat, a men's off-white extra-long pair of 100% cotton thermal underwear size 32, and a library card with Jerry Taylor's signature on it. Jerry took the red plaid coat. The coat had a zipper. Jerry had two choices with clothing, either zipper or snaps. "A one-armed man can't very well button a shirt," he explained when they first met. Jerry wore shoes that were easy to slip on without shoelaces.

But Jerry insisted the other items weren't his. The men's thermal underwear was too narrow and too long for his shorter, rounder body. It wasn't something he wore, and it would be impossible to pull on with one hand. "You know," Jerry said, thinking hard, "Not everyone wears this type of underwear." He looked at Hephzibah straight in the face, "Think hard about who it belongs to." It was men's clothing. It wasn't hers. It didn't belong to Tabitha, Rachel, or anyone at her house. That's all she needed to know. Cotton was comfortable, and the thermal fabric was for warmth. She assumed many men wore them.

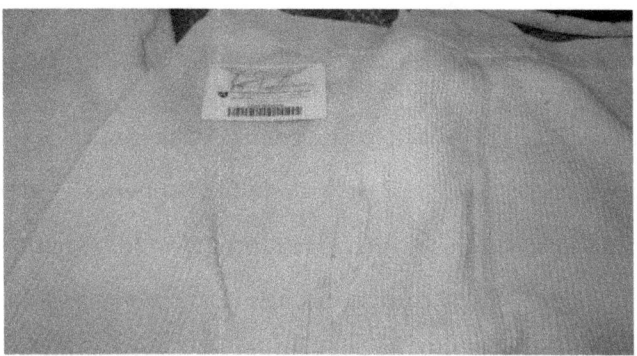

Jerry Taylor's library card, towel, and men's cotton thermal underwear.

Jerry said, "I don't want the library card. I no longer use it," he explained. He wasn't living within walking distance from the library anymore.

Hephzibah complained to herself, "I need Jerry's library card less than I need a large container of black pepper."

She almost tossed the library card in the kitchen garbage. But as a last-minute decision, she put his library card with the men's clothing he didn't take. There was a library just down from his retirement home and the bus took that route. He hadn't discovered it yet. She folded the clothing and gently placed them in the cabinet at the end of the hallway. She was certain those were Jerry's, and he might agree to take them later. Who else could they belong to?

Hephzibah brought out the bath towel for him to take home. Jerry shook his head. She set it near him on the edge of the sofa. She was confused about the bath towel. Maybe she had that wrong. Maybe she was given the towel. She reluctantly put it in the cabinet with the other bath towels.

Jerry started to feel uncomfortable. He asked to go home. Hephzibah moved to take the coat he came with from the hallway closet.

"I'll get my coat," Jerry offered. Hephzibah returned to the kitchen to clean the dishes.

Hephzibah gave Jerry a ride back to the senior apartments. He rode in silence, which wasn't normal for him. He usually turned her car radio down so that they could talk while she drove. He turned the radio volume knob so many turns; it was difficult to turn it back up again. She worried the radio volume might never return. She reminded him to press the power button instead. This time he kept his hand in his lap. He looked as if he did not feel well. He was thinking hard.

When Jerry arrived at his home, he gave Hephzibah a call. "I felt uncomfortable because you were pushing that pink towel on me and it wasn't mine," he explained.

"I accidentally bleached the towel," Hephzibah apologized for the color change. "It used to be blue and turned pink in the wash." The towel remained soft and absorbent. Only the color was affected by the bleach.

"Well, pink or blue," Jerry said, "It wasn't my towel."

"This is confusing," Hepzibah complained. "You accepted the men's red padded coat, and the library card was yours. So, those other items must be yours."

In December, Jerry planned to crash a memorial service at the retirement home for a free dinner. He asked Hephzibah to drive him to Papa Murphy's to pick up a pizza. He purchased a large Cowboy Pizza with Italian sausage, sliced black olives, and mushrooms. He cooked the pizza in his oven. Then he leaned over and peered inside the oven. The oven light lit up his face as he examined the pizza. He used a hand towel to take the pizza out of the oven.

"Do you want me to bring potholders?" Hephzibah asked Jerry. She had plenty of extra potholders at home. She could bring them on the next visit.

"A man with one arm can't very well use oven mitts," he grumbled.

Hephzibah sliced the pizza, and they brought it downstairs to the memorial service.

"Did you know him?" asked a resident about the deceased.

Hephzibah shook her head, "No. I never met the deceased."

"Well, I never," was the resident's response. She was offended at them crashing the memorial service. They left.

"We left the pizza for them to eat," Jerry said. "We did our part."

# 2010

Meeting on January 2010, "We knew erosion would occur, but it is happening faster than we expected. Someone has been digging on the island. When we find out who, there will be hell to pay. The digging on the island is ruining the vegetation," the executive director of the wildlife refuge said at a business meeting. "The only way to get to the island is by boat."

"Or a really good swim," a member responded. He was leaning back in his chair, with his hands crossed behind his head. He had a mischievous grin on his face. The executive director gave him a disapproving glare.

The executive director responded, "No one can swim while carrying a shovel." The mischievous grin melted off of his face. "We are on the lookout for boats. We haven't seen any. So, we think he is traveling at night."

Their conversation caught Hephzibah's attention. She almost squeezed in the comment, "I know someone who can swim while carrying a shovel. He proved he could by tucking a shovel into his pant leg." She may have mentioned the man seen at the marina. But the business meeting conversation moved along without my interruption.

The executive director moved on to talking about the annual plan. There was vegetation they planned to remove and other trees to plant. She explained the reason for the decision, how this would help the habitat, and offered volunteer days to help with planting new trees. There was no discussion at the meeting. She relayed information.

On April 16, 2010, Jerry contacted Hephzibah on Facebook about her garden. He asked her to come to help him plant a garden for himself.

She went to visit him to help him plant a garden in the raised beds outside the apartment complex and to retrieve her Tupperware container. They met another woman who successfully grew many vegetables in the raised beds including tomatoes. Other residents planted flowers. The plants Jerry tried were easier to grow.

Jerry said, "I never had the Tupperware." This was confusing because the Tupperware was missing from Hephzibah's kitchen.

She stood with a frown. "Sit down," Jerry requested. He asked Hephzibah "Is anyone missing the coat I had taken on Thanksgiving? Has anyone asked about it?" He had taken the coat because he liked it. But it wasn't his. Hephzibah wanted to take the coat back or at least take another look at it. She thought she returned the coat to the rightful owner. On the outside she was calm; on the inside, she was panicking. He didn't notice. Jerry said, "I'll hang onto it for now." He didn't move to retrieve it.

The disturbing situation melted with new arrivals at the house. Hephzibah's cat had a litter of kittens and then another litter. The smallest cat of the second litter had her own litter of six kittens. It was a house of laughter. Sterling, the fattest kitten, decided to stand on the toilet seat and sharpen his claws on the toilet paper roll. It was a full roll when he started. Sterling was fascinated to see the roll unravel onto the floor. By the time he became bored, the entire bathroom floor was filled with toilet paper. The grandmother cat looked and motioned to Midnight, the cat from her first litter to peek. Midnight was wide eyed in disbelief. All the cats were sent outside. The cats determined the culprit and shunned him, by sitting with their backs to Sterling. Sterling was sniffling and holding back tears.

Midnight went for a walk around the block. This was his way of patrolling the neighborhood. Velvet, one of the smallest kittens, followed closely behind. Then all the other kittens lined up behind her. Sterling brought up the rear of the line and had to hustle to keep up with the group. Midnight heard the patter of paws behind him and turned to look. He had a surprised look on his face as he saw the six kittens following him away from their home. Velvet looked down with a sheepish look. The entire string of kittens was led back home. Hephzibah and Tabitha snatched them up to keep them from walking away again. Tabitha said, "Midnight walked off much quicker this time." They both laughed. Then the kittens found new homes. Only four cats remained in the house.

Hephzibah kept important telephone numbers on her refrigerator door. This included the telephone numbers of the neighbors. Lee owned the house next door on the east side. It was a double lot. Lee referred to Hephzibah, his "backyard neighbor" and laughed. Lee worked in all branches of the military, Army, Marines, Navy, Coast Guard, and Air Force. He was a useful handyman and was now retired.

Lee received a telephone call from a man who said he was Hephzibah's father. He wanted to check up on her. He wanted to know where she worked, her work schedule, and the times she was gone from the house. Tabitha told Lee not to tell anyone where they worked. However, Lee didn't think this request applied to Hephzibah's father. He determined it was okay to share information with the caring dad.

Later Hephzibah walked into her house and tripped as she was heading into the hallway. There was a pile of DVDs all over the floor in front of the television set. The pile blocked a clear access to the bathroom and bedrooms. Hephzibah preferred movies, so she put them in front. Then the pile would happen again. Hephzibah hadn't noticed the pattern. Hephzibah had so many things to do and so many things on her mind, that it never occurred to her to investigate why the pile of DVDs was there or who was watching her DVDs while she was at work. She assumed it was Tabitha or Rachel.

Tabitha noticed the pattern. The movie DVDs were brought out to access the TV series DVDs in the back. This was the reason for the pile. Tabitha assumed Hephzibah was the one bringing those DVDs forward. One of the "White Collar" DVDs was missing.

Tabitha noticed the TV antenna was moved, and they were both too short to reach it. "Is the TV antenna in a better position or in a worse position for reception?" Hephzibah asked.

"In a better position," Tabitha answered. "We'll just leave it."

The cover for the sofa kept getting out of place. This annoyed Hephzibah too. There was enough cleaning to do without having to constantly put the sofa cover back into place. She wanted the house to look nice. The house was an investment. She would have liked to have guests over. But it was a struggle. She couldn't keep up with cleaning and working to pay the bills.

Mason, one of the kittens, went missing for three days. When he returned, he was bleeding, his left ear was torn, and his right back leg was twisted up, past a ninety-degree angle. Mason didn't want anyone else near him except Hephzibah. Hephzibah didn't know if he was mauled by a raccoon or hit by a car. She consulted the veterinarian.

The veterinarian observed no bite marks on the cat. The cat wasn't mauled by an animal. The injuries weren't consistent with a road accident. A child couldn't have twisted the cat's leg past ninety degrees. A child wouldn't be strong enough. This had to have been done by an adult. The veterinarian angrily demanded to know who in the neighborhood would do this.

Hephzibah recalled the neighbor a block away who has a raccoon for a pet. "He has a son ..." Hephzibah started to answer. The vet was becoming angrier. "I'm sorry," Hephzibah said, "I don't know of anyone else in the neighborhood. He is the only one who is a little off." She told herself it might have been something else. Maybe the vet misunderstood.

Tabitha moved the Kirby vacuum cleaner away from the electric heater. She was worried about the vacuum becoming hot. She opened the hallway closet. Now that the hallway closet door was open, this allowed Mason to show Ebony the floor. Ebony was a cat from the second litter. Ebony looked down and jumped back. Tabitha placed the vacuum cleaner over the trap door to the crawl space below. The cats looked up at her with appreciation. "I think you should keep your vacuum cleaner right here," Tabitha advised Hephzibah. The cats look relieved.

Hephzibah noticed the reaction of the cats. She thought this was strange. She said, "The isn't anything in the closet, except coats." But she agreed with Tabitha to keep the vacuum cleaner in the closet. It made the room tidier. Tabitha thought the cats were relieved because they hated the sound the vacuum made.

Her once very social kitten had become un-socialized. The veterinarian was concerned Mason's panic would give him a heart attack. The kitten was immediately put back into the pet carrier and sent home without an exam and without his vaccines. A veterinary visit now required two tranquilizers to make Mason calm. The prescription for sedation was filled. Even that was not enough. The best veterinarian was unable to calm him down enough for a regular check-up.

Hephzibah was gardening and entered through the front door. She looked down and brushed her feet on the welcome mat. In the kitchen there was mud on the floor. "Who keeps tracking mud in here?" she asked.

Rachel noticed, "There are mud streaks on the floor next to the door."

"Maybe I need to put out a new welcome mat," Hephzibah said as she glanced at the front door. "The old welcome mat is no longer effective at trapping dirt. The mat has gained recognition as a biological habitat. Strawberry plants have found a way to take root there."

"No, the mud streaks are across the kitchen floor next to the door to the garage," Rachel clarified. The individual mud streaks were shaped like triangles, one inch at the base, that extended from the garage door across the kitchen floor about eighteen inches to two feet. The combination of mud streaks spanned two feet wide.

"It looked like arrows pointing to the living room," Hephzibah noted.

"Or pointing to the kitchen hallway," Rachel said. "The mud was wet." There were no recent rains. It looked like something wet and muddy was dragged across the kitchen floor.

Hephzibah's drinking glasses were falling out of the kitchen cupboard. The first was a crystal red wine glass given to her by her sister. Usually, Hephzibah screamed and then caught the item as it was falling. The crystal red wine glass catch was missed, and the glass crashed in shatters on the kitchen counter. Hephzibah blamed Tabitha, but the glass wasn't pushed to the edge. The glass was placed on the edge of the cupboard shelf and then the cupboard door was closed.

Her sister Julia had the same problem at her house. She also let out a scream, but usually caught the glasses before they fell. Julia's husband just let the glasses fall in a crash on the tile kitchen counter when he opened the cupboard door. "We can buy more glasses," he laughed. His wife looked at him with a scared look and flinched.

Hephzibah's father caught the culprit. A visitor was at his house. The visitor went into the kitchen and placed a glass on the very edge of the cupboard shelf and then gently and quietly closed the cupboard door. The set up was intentional. "What are you doing?" Hephzibah's father yelled at him. Later her father complained, "He wasn't even trying to get a drink," but he didn't warn anyone else in the family. He didn't know his daughters were struggling with the same problem at their houses.

## Going Under the Knife

In 2010, Hephzibah, Tabitha, and Rachel received a message from Jerry that he was going under the knife. His ticker wasn't working right, and he needed heart bypass surgery. Only close family members were allowed to visit, but Jerry insisted on seeing us after his surgery was complete. He referred to us as family to the intensive care nurse. We appreciated the comment.

The doctors had to perform double heart bypass surgery. So, it was more of a surgery than what they planned. Jerry was instructed to cough from time to time to clear his lungs. This was to prevent pneumonia from setting in. He had to hold a pillow tight to his chest while coughing. He needed some help with that.

This was the last time we saw Jerry. He left the hospital with an old flame. She came to the ICU while we were there. "He's still pretty special," she said. Three seemed like a crowd, six was indecent. However, she was in another romantic relationship and only stepped in to care for Jerry during his recovery from surgery. Jerry could see her new beau was a "nice guy." He didn't want to shake things up. If we were better friends, we would have been there; it is easy to blame yourself when someone is gone.

At home Rachel asked Hephzibah, "Why do you keep buying that Philly steak flavor of hot pockets?" Rachel closed the freezer door and looked at Hephzibah. There were another two boxes of Philly steak favored hot pockets on the top shelf of the freezer.

"Because when I buy them, I never have a chance to eat them," Hephzibah complained. "They are gone before I've had a chance to try them." They weren't kosher. The beef and cheese combination violated the rule of no meat with dairy. This was a rabbinic rule based on the law of Moses to not seethe a baby goat in its own mother's milk. Hephzibah bought the hot pockets as an indulgence. But that wasn't the issue at this moment. Each time she bought them, they were soon missing.

Rachel looked at Hephzibah in disbelief. Then she looked at Tabitha and asked, "Who would eat them?"

## The Last Invite

When Hephzibah first purchased the house, the home inspector told her, "I found a pile of ant casings. You will need to hire an exterminator." She made a few calls. She located plenty of landscapers, but no exterminators. The request for an exterminator and other small repairs needed to wait until the expertise was available.

In 2012, the Natura Pest Control Company was starting up in the area. This was Hephzibah's first opportunity to hire an exterminator. The pest control company owner found a trail of ants behind the rose bushes to the southeast corner of the house. "There are odiferous ants and field ants," he said. "You have both." He pointed with his spray gun, "The ants found something to eat right here," the exterminator said.

Hephzibah bent down to take a closer look and then surveyed the overall position of the house. "This room is furthest from the kitchen," she responded. "This is just a location they found to gain entrance to the house."

"No," the exterminator insisted. "There are many places the ants can gain entrance to the house. They've found something to eat here."

Hephzibah searched in the bedroom above. There was no food. There were also no ants. This was puzzling. It created some burning questions. Where were the ants going? And what did they find to eat?

Eventually, Hephzibah's cleaning concentrated on smell mitigation. She just focused on washing the laundry, eight loads a week, and doing the dishes. These were things she could accomplish. The plan to have visitors over to a clean house was out of reach.

A black short-hair cat named Midnight came into Hephzibah's bedroom and meowed. She looked at him, "Hi, Midnight." He meowed again. She turned to look at him, "Do you have something to show me?"

Midnight turned his head to the left. Hephzibah followed him into the kitchen. There was a thick swarm of field ants three feet wide going after the cat food. Hephzibah looked around and found two cans of Raid Ant Spray on the kitchen counter near the sink. She hadn't put the cans there, but she grabbed a can, shook it according to the directions and leapt to the far side of the kitchen, near the door. There she sprayed the ants and then opened the door to continue spraying. Hephzibah expected an ant trail through the garage.

Tabitha looked too. However, they only found a crack in the cement that went under the house. Tabitha said, "They came from under here."

Hephzibah took a closer look at the crack in the cement and glanced over at the driveway. She tried to remember when she bought the cans of Raid. Maybe it was when she was at Albertsons. There was an end aisle display at the grocery store. It must have caught her eye. But, no, she passed by the display. She didn't buy the Raid.

Hephzibah told Rachel, "Thank you for buying the cans of Raid and putting them on the kitchen counter." Even though Hephzibah preferred things to be put away in the cabinet, this time it was handy to have the spray close at hand, on the counter. Hephzibah assumed Rachel picked up the spray when they were grocery shopping at Albertsons. Hephzibah offered to reimburse Rachel, opened her purse and wallet, and tried to hand her $6.00.

But Rachel shook her head. She told Hephzibah, "I didn't put it there. You must have." She didn't accept the money. Rachel left through the front door.

Hephzibah asked Tabitha about the spray. Tabitha shook her head, "No, you must have put it there." She paused and looked back at the cans. "How did they get there?" she asked.

The bottle of dish soap that stood near the kitchen sink slowly drained empty. Hephzibah assumed Tabitha washed the dishes by hand or did a prewash before putting them into the dishwasher. She congratulated her on helping to clean by hand washing the dishes. Hephzibah let her know she could use the automatic dishwasher without a prewash.

Tabitha could not understand why Hephzibah assumed that she hand washed the dishes. Tabitha said, "I never touch the dish soap. Why do you buy it? The automatic dishwasher soap is enough."

Hephzibah went to clean out the garage. She spotted an orange life vest. "Where did this life vest come from?" Hephzibah asked Rachel. The life vest was orange and like the ones loaned out for free down at the marina. The life vest was to be returned after use.

Rachel said, "I don't know." She never went to the marina.

Later Rachel said to Hephzibah, "The life vest is wet. Look!" Tabitha went to look. "Someone went into the garage, used the life vest and then brought it back."

Much later Rachel said, "Now there are two life vests." The new life vest was olive green and lying on the shelf.

Rachel noted, "Sometimes the life vests are hanging on the clothes rack." She glanced back at the garage, "And sometimes they are lying somewhere else in the garage." The life vests don't move by themselves.

Later Rachel said, "One life vest is wet; and the other is dry."

Tabitha had a worried look, "Even I admit that's strange."

Hephzibah responded, "Maybe one takes more time to dry than the other." But she wondered, "Where did these life vests come from?" No one in the house used them. It was too disturbing.

A man at the synagogue reported random things appearing at his house. "Strange things appear at my house all the time," he told Hephzibah. "I have no idea where they came from. Don't worry about it." Neither Hephzibah, Tabitha nor Rachel had spoken with him about the problem. They were unsure how he knew.

Pat was a neighbor who lived on the other side of Lee. Tabitha met Pat when Hephzibah was caught in traffic on the way home. Tabitha introduced him to her family. Rachel stopped in to see him too. He had a very large TV and enjoyed watching the History Channel.

Pat walked his beagle, Danny, down by the kayak launch. It was his dog's highlight of the day. They were getting back in Pat's car. Pat drove to the spot to exercise, even though it wasn't far to walk. Pat saw Hephzibah at the waterfront. He noticed the expression on her face as she saw him open his car and asked her, "You drive down here sometimes, don't you?" He pointed, "I see your car parked down here in the early morning, usually on Friday morning."

Tabitha worked on Friday mornings, and Hephzibah slept in, since she didn't work on Fridays. Hephzibah shook her head. She was about to say, "No, I've never parked here. It wasn't my car."

Pat interrupted Hephzibah's thought by adding, "I noticed the license plate. You'd better head home. I'm going home too." He tugged the leash, "Come on Danny." The beagle obediently hopped onto the blanketed back seat. He assumed Hephzibah wanted to confront Tabitha about driving her car.

There were other things Hephzibah could confront Tabitha about. There was dirt left in the back seat of Hephzibah's car, on the left side of the back car seat. Not just dirt but leaves and stems. She shook her head. Putting a blanket on the backseat of her car, like Pat did for his beagle, was almost tempting. Hephzibah thought, "How can a girl be so dirty? There was dirt left in the bathtub, chunky dirt and more leaf stems." Hephzibah thought, "Tabitha often leaves the front gate open."

On Monday morning, Hephzibah's Pontiac the driver's car seat was moved too far forward. "Did I adjust it here?" she asked herself. She adjusted the seat to the best position for her and never changed it. There was a second adjustment for the driver's car seat that adjusted it up and down, instead of forward and back. Hephzibah never thought about moving the seat up or down. The car salesman adjusted the seat height to fit her size and she never changed it. She thought, "I didn't place the car seat there. It was moved from the ideal position, forward a notch. Was that Tabitha?" She couldn't figure out how to move the car seat back to the original position. She put an ice pack at her back and screamed in pain while driving down the freeway. She complained, "I want to rip the seat out. It wasn't this uncomfortable when I bought it." She didn't notice the seat was lower. A taller person drove her car. Tabitha is shorter, not taller. It wasn't Tabitha. Finally, the fuel tank failed, and she got rid of the Pontiac.

Items were shifting in Tabitha's trunk. Her boots were shoved to the far right. "The bottom line is, I need my boots for work. And I need to be able to get to them," Tabitha complained.

Hephzibah, Tabitha, and Rachel each had their own hook near the door for their car keys. Hepzibah noticed Tabitha's keys showing up on her hook. Hephzibah decided to pick her battles and endured the inconvenience. It was Tabitha who complained to Hephzibah, "Why do you keep putting my keys on your hook?" she asked with irritation.

Hephzibah took a closer look and said quietly, "I was about to ask you the same thing." She looked at Tabitha, "I'll move the keys over to your hook if I find them on mine." But she suspected someone borrowed their cars.

The visitor at Hephzibah's parents' house received a scolding, "What is all this about not putting food in the trunk?" Hephzibah's mother asked.

"That was about the Pontiac," Hephzibah's father said. "He says that as if he knows what is in the trunk more than they do."

"Tabitha's car trunk too," Hephzibah's mother clarified with irritation.

Hephzibah's flashlights kept dying. The flashlight batteries ran down, even without use. This happened with flashlights in the garage, regardless of type, in the house, large and very small, in the kitchen, and in her car. Hephzibah replaced the flashlights' batteries, made sure they were turned off, and that nothing could accidentally turn the flashlights on. Still, it was no use. She threw many flashlights away assuming they were defective. The box of flashlights she used at work was missing.

There was mosquito netting in the garden shed. Rachel said, "This netting belongs to Noelle," a friend of hers. "Don't throw it away," Rachel requested. Later Rachel informed them, "It isn't Noelle's. She has hers." Whose was it? And how did it get here?

The lieutenant was a man who served in the Navy for 19 years. Most of that time he was at sea. He was tall, pale skinned, with blue eyes. His last trip was to Afghanistan. The enemy threw a hand grenade, and it picked up his jeep like a rag doll. His jeep landed upside down on the side of the road. He didn't have visible wounds, only those inside his head. He was retired now and came to visit at Hephzibah's house and noticed weathering on her shovel. "You should keep the shovel in the garage."

"I do that, and I can't find the shovel again," Hephzibah explained, "It is always in a different spot." She kept the shovel in the shed with the gardening supplies, until two men at the marina told her to keep her shovel in the garage. She kept the shovel in the corner near the garage door, but then had headaches trying to locate the shovel again each time she needed it. She was a creature of habit and didn't move things around. "Since the shovel has been kept here, I haven't had a hard time locating it." This was opposite from what the two men at the marina suggested. But that conversation was long forgotten.

Sometimes the shovel was wet. "Was the roof leaking?" she wondered. "I hired a man to inspect the roof, and he found places to upgrade, but not any near the shovel."

"There's something about the way that it's weathered," the lieutenant pondered. The light yellow paint was worn off. The glue in the plywood handle was gone. The handle was swollen, but smooth with no splinters.

"I had three shovels. This one was the best of the three," Hephzibah explained to the lieutenant. "It was painted light yellow with lacquer over the top." The paint and lacquer were long gone.

The lieutenant looked closely at the shovel handle and moved his gaze up and down it. "Someone soaked it in hot, soapy water," the lieutenant determined. Nineteen years of Navy experience can't be wrong.

Tabitha admitted, "I use the garden hoe to keep down weeds, but I never use the shovel." The garden hoe was in perfect condition and had no weathering, with the red painted handle as good as new, not even a chip in the paint. Tabitha always returned it to the garden shed. Tabitha wasn't the problem.

"How do you get the shed door open?" Hephzibah asked. For a long time, Hephzibah had been unable to budge the shed door. It was stuck shut. She pulled on the door with all her strength, trying to get it to open. She often gave up putting things away. Glass canning jars stayed in a pile near the kitchen sink, because she couldn't open the shed door to put them away.

"I just open it," Tabitha answered. "I usually open it in the late afternoon."

Hephzibah tried in the early morning. This was the time she started her cleaning. Rise early and start cleaning before other interruptions occur. This was her formula for cleaning. The time of day the shed door is opened shouldn't make a difference. It is just a sliding door.

The lieutenant turned his attention to the bullet holes in Hephzibah's bedroom window. He confirmed her suspicion that the lower bullet hole was from a BB gun. For the upper bullet hole, he made a careful inspection. He backed up and then moved in again, closing one eye and squinting. "This bullet hole has the bullet spray of a pellet gun," he said. "Maybe from a distance." He glanced behind him. There wasn't much distance. He took another look and confirmed his first statement. No one else could answer that question.

Hephzibah returned to college for a graduate degree. She attended math courses and was at the top of her class. The lieutenant wasn't around anymore. His absence left an opening. Problems started at the house. The toilet was clogged when Hephzibah came home. She had to unclog the toilet before preparing dinner. She was already in a rush without this extra chore, and it happened a few times. There was no explanation for who clogged the toilet.

Rachel found another problem. "The bras on the clothes rack are wet," Rachel said as she came in through the door between the garage and the kitchen. The rack was a white metal drying rack for clothing. It stood in the garage. "I think something is happening to them as they dry on the rack." She paused. "I'm just noticing. They don't dry very fast." She referred to undergarments hanging to dry after the delicate wash. They were taking days to dry. "I think it has something to do with the life jackets being on the same rack." Rachel noted, "The bras seem to become wetter the longer they hang on the rack."

This hardly seemed possible. Either the life jackets caused a damp garage which transferred to the clothing, or the appearance of the life jackets coincided with the wetness of the bras. But the odor never fully went away. The longer they hung to dry in the garage, the worse they smelled. For some reason a double wash barely helped. Bras had to be worn and dry or not, they were grabbed off the rack, worn once, and tossed back into the laundry to be washed again. Hephzibah hoped frequently washing the bras would help with the odor.

Hephzibah's bras hung on the line to dry. Dry or not, she had to wear them if other bras were in the laundry. Hephzibah wore the bras once and washed them again, but that didn't help reduce the smell. Tabitha didn't have this problem, because she put her bras in the dryer.

A man told Hephzibah's mother, "After someone ejaculates on her bras, she just puts them on and wears them again." He chuckled.

Hephzibah's mother said, "What a nasty girl." But she didn't communicate with Hephzibah about it. Hephzibah's mother confessed to Julia, her older daughter, "I'm missing part of the big picture."

Julia replied to her mother, "You're missing all of the big picture."

Hephzibah worked hard to try to find out who her parents were speaking with. She noticed something was off. Every time she asked her parents, they clammed up. It was disturbing.

"I wish I could blame this on someone else," Hephzibah mourned to herself, "especially after I criticized Lee for giving out information about my work schedule to a stranger over the telephone." She received a telephone call from a stranger.

The telephone caller seemed like a nice person. He struck up a casual conversation and put her at ease. He asked me, "You might know this, who is Jerry Taylor?"

She provided information about who Jerry was, politely answering his questions. She was taught to be polite more than she was taught to tell strangers to shove off. This is a failing. It's hard to admit that being polite can be a failing.

"Is there anything of Jerry's that you like," the caller asked.

"I like the way he hangs his spider plants using his black supports. It creates an inviting atmosphere in the apartment," Hephzibah answered. She didn't mention that she enjoys the quirky way Jerry found a way to use the supports that act as his left arm. That was too much unnecessary information. Jerry achieved the inviting atmosphere with live plants and lighting from indirect sunlight. She admired his hospitality.

It was mid-July 2015 in the late afternoon. The days were sunny and hot. Jerry called Hephzibah on the telephone, "A group of us are going down to the lake," Jerry said. The statement had an informative tone. Jerry's usual excitement was missing. There wasn't a familiar, "Hey", at the beginning of the announcement. It was off and not exactly an invite.

"Which lake?" Hephzibah asked. She wondered if he needed transportation. Maybe that was the reason for the call.

"The one in the city," Jerry responded. There was no public bus to this location. The lake was best reached by car.

"Oh, that one," Hephzibah responded. "That's across town." She wondered how he planned to get there.

"It's not that far," Jerry assured. "Only about five miles," he calculated. "Depending on which side of the lake you go to."

Hephzibah didn't know much about the lake. It seemed to only have one public access area. She went there for a birthday party many years ago. The automatic sprinklers came on in the picnicking area and drowned the food. She wondered if the lake access changed. Usually there is less access over time instead of more, as housing developments sprout up. "Were you wanting me to go?" she asked. The reason for Jerry's call might be an invitation for her to join. But his vocal tone didn't fit. His original excitement quickly faded.

"No," Jerry replied hesitantly. "No," Jerry said definitively. It was almost a warning. The voice tone was the way you'd tell a dog to "Stay." Jerry's voice tone returned to normal, "Hey, there's a guy here who says he knows you."

"Um," Hephzibah responded. "Okay?" It seemed doubtful. The only person who might be in Jerry's area was George, who was arrested for child molestation. George had a conversation with Hephzibah at the Peach Tree Restaurant. Child Protective Services overheard their conversation and intervened. George or someone else, either way this sounded alarming.

Jerry said, "He will drive us to the lake in his truck. He has floatation devices for us to use, in a white plastic sack."

Hephzibah thought of floatation devices as water toys, inflatables, and noodles. She imagined a man sitting with a large bag and pool toys spilling out the top. Something seemed off. Any angle Hephzibah looked at it, this couldn't be good. She started to express her hesitation, "Ah, …"

Jerry cut her off in mid-sentence, "Well, see you soon," he said. The statement itself was cheerful. But he was not his honest self. Again, the familiar "Hey" was missing from his comment. He didn't add an excited," Woo Hoo," after saying, "See you soon."

Hephzibah stepped out onto the front porch. She sat on the wooden bench leaning forward and looking towards the water, with her hands resting under her thighs. She was positioned to push off the bench, as she watched the sun go down. Something wasn't right. Everything was dark, so it was too late for a trip to the lake; the park would close at dusk. Hephzibah began to feel guilty, but she had never learned how to swim, so the deep-water lake was not entirely safe for her. "Is it safe for Jerry?" she asked herself. She had never known Jerry to back down from a fight.

Hephzibah listened intently. Usually there was the sound of crickets down by the water, coyotes howling, or the rustle of trees. Tonight, there was not a sound. The wildlife refuge was too quiet, deathly quiet.

She gave Jerry a call on his cell phone. There was no answer. Hesitantly she opened the garage door and peeked inside. The life jackets that mysteriously came and went out of her garage were in a white plastic grocery sack yesterday. Today the life jackets were gone. She had a sinking feeling and called 911.

The 911 responder asked, "How old is Jerry?" The responder told her not to worry. "Jerry is a big man and can take care of himself," she assured Hephzibah. "He told you not to come along and you did what he asked," the responder said. "That is all you can do." She hung up the phone.

Two days later the life jackets reappeared in the garage. They were out of the white plastic bag and lying on the floor. Hephzibah might have checked if they were wet, but she couldn't go near them. She couldn't even step into the garage. She closed the garage door and sat down in silence. Her hands were folded in her lap. At times like these she really needed a good sound board. Important puzzle pieces were missing.

## Wrapped in Mosquito Netting

In the fall, Hephzibah took the bus home from the city. A homeless man rode the bus, too. He said to the bus driver, "I planned to ride as far north as possible and then continue to walk north."

The bus driver stopped at Hephzibah's house. The homeless man asked to exit with Hephzibah. Hephzibah shook her head at the bus driver. The homeless man stopped in fear, "Wait," he said. "This is where you live? I don't want to stop there. Word gets around." He looked at Hephzibah and warned, "You don't want to exit there either. You should be frightened." The bus driver took the homeless man back to the transit center.

The household was going through two full gallons of milk per week, and that was with Hephzibah cutting back on her milk. This continued after Rachel moved to Colorado. One less person in the house didn't change the milk consumption. Each week Hephzibah bought a gallon of nonfat and a gallon of reduced fat milk. Each week the gallons were used up. Tabitha said, "I only drink the nonfat milk." This didn't explain why the reduced fat milk was used up.

In mid-December 2015, Hephzibah was in pain. It hurt to lie down. It hurt to sit. It hurt to stand. It had hurt to run. So, she decided to take a walk. She planned to walk until it hurt too bad to take a step. All she could do to keep out of unmanageable pain was walk. She walked up the ridge and back down again. The sky was clear and stars were visible. The winter air was cold and crisp. The cold helped her feel better. She walked two miles. She went into the backyard, only to extend her walk.

Three raccoons were outside just east of the shed, munching on discarded squash. The raccoons weren't what frightened her so badly. The garden shed door was open, those doors were opened in such a way Hephzibah could not have been able to open them. The right door that always sticks shut was halfway open. The left door, which was the only one that moved, was closed. There was something large and white inside. There was a noise in the shed, two heavy stomps, steps too heavy for a raccoon. It wasn't a bear. White bears are polar bears. She wasn't in the Arctic. It was too thin for a bear. Too tall for much else. Hephzibah went into medical shock and ran inside in house.

There was a tall man in the garden shed wrapped head to toe in white mosquito netting. He was stomping on ants with his tennis shoes. "Sometimes I feel like the ants are going to overtake me," he confessed to a friend. "But I'm finding time to sleep." His friend wondered where he was staying. "My only thought is to give them something else to eat."

Hephzibah met weekly with a math professor at the college. When she was called in by the student conduct board, she had no idea what they were referring to. They only gave her a copy of the student manual and no other clue to her offense. The "witnesses" who were with the professor contacted Hephzibah as she exited the library. They said, "We don't know what we heard, and no one saw anything." They said, "There was no one outside the professor's window."

On April 22, 2016, Hephzibah and Tabitha prepared for Passover. This was a peaceful time of year with only one focus. All leaven was removed. The house was cleaned. Tabitha was talented at reviewing the most recent rabbinic laws on what was Passover kosher. Fence laws changed from year to year. Together they worked to clear all the hametz (food with leaven) out of the kitchen. Tabitha then hid it in the garage. This year the teriyaki sauce needed to go. Hephzibah put all the refrigerated items into a cooler, although she knew the food might not last until the end of Passover. By the week of Passover week, the garage smelled like teriyaki sauce. The cooler, which Hephzibah secured shut, was open a crack.

Hephzibah was expelled from the college for stalking, when she was the one stalked. Some of the comments suggested a person she had a protection order against. When she was at the main campus ten years prior, she was able to put a block on her account to deter domestic abuse. At the satellite campus, a block was unavailable. Why are personal comments part of a Student Conduct Board hearing? Why was someone allowed to do this anonymously? Her grades were good. Professors referred to her as a top student. People now assumed her grades were poor. Nothing made sense.

In October 2016, Hephzibah had a pipe burst. Water soaked the carpet in the hallway. The plumbers drilled for another pipe and found digging below Tabitha's room too big to be an animal. Tabitha began to have a reaction to the mold, so Hephzibah ripped up the carpet. The floorboards in the hallway were now exposed. One of the floorboards was lifted out of position. She could see a gap that had not been there before.

Hephzibah took a service technician position. The new job kept her on the road most of the time. Memorial Day weekend 2017, her lodging was rented out for a special country music event. She needed to go home on Friday after work, instead of waiting until Saturday morning to make the return trip.

At this same time, Tabitha accepted a friend's request to go to the beach. She left on Friday afternoon. Rachel remained in Colorado.

When Hephzibah returned home, she was tired and went straight to bed. But it was hard to sleep. There was a digging sound, the sound of a shovel chipping against cement. She dreamt of an Italian man with thick black hair matted with blood on the left side. In the morning, someone closed her bedroom door. She saw a pale arm, longer than Tabitha's, close her door. But she reasoned it was Tabitha. Who else would it be? She saw the Kirby vacuum cleaner placed in Tabitha's room.

When Tabitha returned home, she confessed that she left with friends for the beach on Friday. She thought Hephzibah put the Kirby in her room as a suggestion to vacuum. Hephzibah was alarmed to realize that neither of them put the Kirby in Tabitha's room. And Tabitha wasn't the one who closed Hephzibah's bedroom door.

There was an odor in Hephzibah's room. Opening the window didn't help. Maybe the smell was outside. The rotting cabbage smell is so strong it sticks to your teeth and the roof of your mouth when you breathe it in.

In 2018 Hephzibah returned home after a business trip. The kitchen counter was full of dirty dishes and empty milk jugs, which could not be rinsed out in the sink, because the sink was full of dirty dishes. The dirty dishes could not be placed into the dishwasher, because the dishwasher was full of clean dishes. The dishwasher could not be emptied, because the dirty dishes on the kitchen counter were piled too high to gain access to the kitchen cupboards.

Tabitha responded, "It would help if you cleaned up before you leave."

Hephzibah responded, "I do clean up before I leave." Coming home after a business trip was hardly a break. There was so much housework to do, it was exhausting. After each trip home, she was eager to return to work.

"What's with the bag of lotions?" Rachel asked. She was back for a visit.

Hephzibah thought Rachel referred to a small bag of lotions she collected during her business trips. She put the lotions in a small toothbrush bag. The small bag was in her bedroom closet. "You mean those bags you receive at the dentist when they give you a new toothbrush?" Hephzibah asked, confused.

Rachel clarified, "No, the red bag that is in the garden shed. It is a zippered overnight bag."

"You mean the large red suitcase that has quilts in it?" Hephzibah asked. "The burgundy one with rollers and a pull handle?" Hephzibah turned, looked towards her car and said, "Wait, that can't be in the shed." That suitcase was in the trunk of her car. "I use the large suitcase for business trips," she said in confusion.

"No," Rachel said. "The red bag in the garden shed. Go take a look."

Hephzibah went to the shed to look. There were lotions and gels of every type and scent. There was an anal sex vibrator. Jerry's library card stuck to the inside. Hephzibah assumed the red bag was Jerry's. "I really don't know what Jerry was in to," Hephzibah murmured. She put the bag back into the shed. If she had an opportunity to see him, she planned to return the items. She would insist he take them.

It was mid-October 2019. Hephzibah had a date with Alfredo. She hadn't seen him in years. She met him when she worked as an electrical engineer at Remedial Action Schemes. When they first met, he was passing through a festival and looking for a place to sit down. All the tables were occupied. She invited him over to her table to eat. His English was much better now than when Hephzibah initially met Alfredo, although he used the word, "olweitz" instead of "always." It was one word he never got right. But it was endearing.

For their date, Hephzibah met him at the post office and rode with him in his truck down to the kayak launch. They kissed. He ran his hand up her thigh and under her dress. They decided to go for a walk to find a secluded place. They passed by a couple sitting on the rocks facing the river.

"It looks like you have the same idea we do," Alfredo said. They traveled past the rocks down to where the fishermen cast their lines. Alfredo shook his head at the first sandy beach and opted for the second. Tree branches obscured their activity.

The place was wetter than usual after the September rains. There was a place where a fire was made. Charred wood was in a scattered pile. An energy drink aluminum can was left behind in the fire pit. Someone spent time here. Not a homeless person. There was no shelter, no fabric. The fire pit looked wrong. There was scattered sand, as if someone was digging and tossing the sand randomly. High tide leveled the sand. So, the digging was before the last high tide. Before the water washes away our sins, it exposes them. Here along the bank, water exposed severed tree roots.

Later in the week, Hephzibah noticed there was thick clear plastic in the garage. She saw this plastic off and on. It seemed to come and go, like the life vests. Was it left by the previous owner of the house? Were they doing their own painting? There were no paint drips on the plastic. Hephzibah thought, "They must be meticulous. I'd have drips everywhere. It must be a failing." She left the plastic to use as a drip cloth when she painted. But when she tried to find the plastic for painting, it wasn't there. At Miller Paint, the only plastic they had was very thin. She purchased it. The plastic was spotted with light brown paint. The light brown splattered plastic lay on the floor in the garage and never moved. The thicker plastic came and went in and out of the garage. The thicker plastic was folded with military skill, always on the crease. The thicker plastic remained clean but must have been used because it appeared from nowhere.

I told Hephzibah, "I tried to find this type of plastic at the paint store, but they didn't sell it. I saw this type of plastic once before. Long ago when I recently divorced. I opened the trunk of my Chevrolet Nova to clean it out. I was positioned near the dumpster when I looked down and paused, but I wasn't sure if I wanted to know. I froze in my stance." I continued to describe the scene:

A man came up behind me and peered over my shoulder. He said, "From the way you were looking down, I could tell." I looked as if I viewed a crime scene. He moved into position for inspection. "The plastic is thick, and quadruple folded. There is no dirt. It is completely wiped clean. Whatever he was doing, he wasn't taking any chances. From the size of the plastic, I'd say large drug shipments. That's my final guess." He looked at me, "Are you going to call the police?"

"For what?" I asked him. "To tell them I found plastic in my trunk?" Large drug shipments didn't fit. But it was true, the plastic had no dirt and meticulously no fingerprints. It was wiped clean, which was odd for something in a car trunk. I pulled the plastic out of my trunk and tossed it into the dumpster. The trunk carpet was unaffected. "I expected to see stains," I admitted. I sighed in relief.

Hephzibah stepped over the thinner paint splattered plastic crumpled on the garage floor. She kept this story in mind. Then she looked over at the thicker plastic folded with military corners. She shook her head as she contemplated tossing the thinner plastic. She thought, "Obviously he doesn't want that one." Part of her came to the realization that someone was going into the garage. Locking the garage door wasn't much help. The intruder cracked the door frame to get in.

In the garden shed Tabitha found one California king seafoam green satin comforter and a brown sleeping bag. Tabitha told Hephzibah the items belonged to Lee. Later Hephzibah pulled the lawnmower out of the garden shed. She was in a hurry to complete her chores.

"That isn't mine," Lee said as he ran over to Hephzibah. At first Hephzibah thought Lee was talking about the lawn mower. Lee was referring to the comforter and sleeping bag. "I haven't been watching the house. But I will now," he promised. He was very concerned and ruffled.

Hephzibah also found a green and gold plaid blanket. She assumed the plaid blanket was Jerry's. She was disappointed to not locate the true owner of the items. The sleeping bag in the garden shed painted a very real picture of what was going on. She missed it. Somehow the sleeping bag didn't look out of place with the other camping gear.

A foul smell was coming from the raised floorboard in the hallway. The floorboard wasn't raised when she purchased the property. The real estate agent had her shuffle her feet down the hallway to show how level the foundation was. That was impossible now. And it wasn't a sinking floor.

The boards measured perfectly level at each end. And one board in the middle of the hallway was at an angle. Someone was below her.

If Hephzibah had stopped to think about the chain of events, she might have solved it. But a large piece of the puzzle was missing. For a very long time, her mother accused her of being paranoid or hyper-sensitive to stalking. She was encouraged to dismiss things that were clues. The food missing from the refrigerator, the snacks missing from the kitchen cupboard, were all clues. The garage back door was left open. The side door double locked. She told herself it was something else. Gaslighting.

Hephzibah looked up at the ceiling in her bathroom. There were brown spots on the ceiling above the shower. Two visits from the professional house cleaners showed no improvement in the spots. Alfredo looked at the ceiling and told her, "A tall man was using your shower," he said, "Someone taller than me." He sat back down on the sofa and gave her a questioning look. She was someone he couldn't trust. Hephzibah looked back at him and gently shook her head. He left.

Hephzibah's shampoo bottle was moved to a shelf below its usual location. She had asked Tabitha to use her own shampoo, but Tabitha was. The shampoo continued to move. Hephzibah's bath towel that hung to dry was just as wet at the end of the day.

Tabitha asked Hephzibah, "Why do you keep closing your door?" The door to Hephzibah's bedroom was closed.

"I don't close the door," Hephzibah answered. "I'm always afraid there will be a cat in there, and I don't have a litter box."

"That's why I opened it," Tabitha explained. A black ball of fur gave her an appreciative glance. She asked, "Do you want a litter box?"

"No," Hephzibah answered.

## December 31, 2020

Hephzibah was lying in bed. It was dark outside, as dark as black ink. It was in the wee hours of the morning in December. It was so late in the year that was almost New Year's Day. In less than 24 hours they would bring out the noise makers and party hats. Hephzibah's quilts and her coffee brown comforter were pulled up over her shoulders to stay warm. She laid on her back and tried to sleep.

Outside Hephzibah's window there was a series of sounds. The first sound was a sound that lowered in pitch as it moved, like a jet plane flying at high speed through the air. But it was a few octaves higher than a jet, smaller, and much closer to the ground. The sound traveled north northwest and lowered in altitude as it moved.

The second sound was Ebony meowing. This was a loud, low meow. The meow indicated, "Come quick, something is wrong" or "I am in pain." At this noise, Hephzibah anticipated she would find the cat injured or attacked. Ebony was a large cat, part Maine coon. He was timid in his kitten years, scared of his own shadow. The snowstorm came in. He was lost in the forest for two weeks in the snow. He survived by learning to catch his food and by learning to beg. He managed to find his way back home. When he found his way back to the front door, he dashed into the house and dashed under Tabitha's bed. Tabitha was so delighted to find him. "It looks like Ebony", Tabitha said, "It is Ebony." Over the years, Ebony became brave. Tabitha said, "He finally realized that he is bigger than the other cats."

The third sound was of metal sliding over gravel. There was an imperfect echo to the sound. The sound was a low pitch. Whatever moved had weight to it. Hephzibah expected the sound of a crash would follow, but it didn't.

The fourth sound was aluminum sliding in an arc across wood. This sound was on the side of the house; it started about five feet high and moved towards the north and arced downwards towards the ground. The arc was that of a circle and the pivot was about 40 degrees.

The fifth sound was the sound of aluminum bouncing twice on the concrete. The object bouncing was long and narrow. Ebony made no noise at these sounds. Somehow that made them more frightening. If Ebony was near these last three sounds, why didn't he meow again?

And finally, the last sound was a flapping sound. Did Ebony grow bird wings and his wings were flapping? No, the flapping sound went towards the south southeast. There were three flaps. It was the sound of three footsteps running towards the fenced backyard. The footsteps flapped from heel to toe. Hephzibah knew that sound. The person was a man, wearing large canvas tennis shoes with a flexible sole. Why would a man run to the backyard instead of to the front? He didn't leave the property. What did he do that caused the noises? Why didn't he leave? Why was he still there?

Hephzibah grabbed her flashlight. Ebony's meow indicated for her to come quickly. She couldn't trust light to come from any electrical switch. Attempts to rely on an overhead light led to disappointment. The outdoor motion sensor light was busted out. The garage light often failed to work. The light flickered in the broken light fixture and faded to dark. She learned to view overhead lights as pathetic and failing when needed the most. The flashlight was the only light source.

Hephzibah opened the garage door to the backyard. Tabitha rose out of bed and came up behind Hephzibah. Hephzibah shined her flashlight on the cat who was huddled under the BBQ. That was what caused the third sound. The legs of the BBQ sliding across the gravel on the patio. "I'm afraid to go out there," Hephzibah admitted. Her muscles were frozen.

"Why?" Tabitha asked. "It's just Ebony." She moved past Hephzibah in the doorway and walked towards her cat. She stooped low with bent knees.

"Right," Hephzibah mumbled, "It's just Ebony," Her muscles remained frozen.

Ebony was trying to move towards Tabitha. He could only drag the BBQ with him. This created the sound of metal sliding over gravel. His round yellow owl-like eyes were focused on Tabitha and pleading for help.

"There I something wrong with him," Hephzibah pointed out. She wanted to move the flashlight around the area to see what else was there, to see what caused this. But she couldn't. She was too afraid of what she would find. She concentrated on Ebony. The third sound was solved. "I don't think he can move his legs," Hephzibah told Tabitha. Maybe that was the reason for the flapping noise. Maybe she imagined the canvas tennis shoes.

"Of course he can move his legs," Tabitha answered indignantly. Tabitha bent down and picked up the cat. She let out a dismayed gasp. She held the cat close to her as she rushed him into the house. She sat down in the rocker with Ebony in her arms. She moved into taking charge. "We need to take him to the vet," Tabitha said.

There was no arguing with her. "Even the animal hospital is closed until 8:00 a.m.," Hephzibah observed. It wasn't a disagreement, just an obstacle. "Where can we take him at this hour?" Hephzibah asked Tabitha. "Is there someplace in the city?" she asked. "Some veterinarians might be closed for the holiday."

"Oh, no, they won't be closed," Tabitha said. She was determined. She looked around. "Is there a phone book?" Tabitha asked.

Hephzibah looked down at the floor and dived for the yellow pages. She flipped through to "V" for veterinarian. She sat down on the sofa and concentrated. She looked for anything that might be open during off hours.

"That's what I needed you to do," Tabitha said. Now Tabitha pulled out her phone to do her own search. Together they explored the options. The goal was to find whichever vet hospital that could take him first. This they agreed on. Distance was a factor only if it delayed the time he would receive help. Tabitha selected a hospital nearby.

Hephzibah ran to get the pet carrier. Tabitha objected, "There is no way to get Ebony in the carrier." Hephzibah scooped up the cat and slipped him in. Tabitha pursed her lips together in frustration. Usually getting Ebony into a pet carrier took days of careful, skillful planning. "I was just going to hold him," Tabitha explained. Hephzibah placed a dark blue blanket over the pet carrier, and they waited. The veterinarian would be open to receive him at 7:00 a.m.

The mother cat came out to see Ebony. "She's keeping him calm," Tabitha said. There was a forced calm throughout the room. When it was time to go, Hephzibah drove. Tabitha provided directions.

"I don't think there is a veterinarian down here," Tabitha objected.

"Oh, yes there is," Tabitha countered. "Just pull in."

The office was small, cool, and dimly lit, tall plants surrounded the room. The veterinarian asked, "Who is the owner of the cat?" She focused on calming Tabitha who was in tears. There was no visible open wound, no blood. Ebony's legs were cold and had no pulse. There was a blood clot in his lower back. The clot stopped the blood flow to his back legs.

"There is no sign of blunt force trauma," Hephzibah said. There was no open wound.

"Except for the blood clot," the veterinarian corrected. "The blood clot can be caused by a variety of things from illness to a blunt force." The veterinarian looked intently at Tabitha, "Ebony is in pain." The veterinarian couldn't save him and recommended euthanizing the cat.

They brought Ebony home in a cardboard coffin. Hephzibah grabbed the shovel that was kept next to the garden window. She approached the BBQ. The garden hoe was lying next to the BBQ at the side of the house. This is what made the sound of aluminum sliding in an arc. And the sound of aluminum bouncing on concrete. "I should have put the hoe away," Hephzibah said regretfully.

The hoe was lying in the wrong direction. Ebony was injured from the back, not from the front. The hoe had a wooden handle. The sound wasn't the handle sliding in an arc. Only the end of the hoe was aluminum. "When was the last time you used the hoe?" Tabitha asked. She asked because she couldn't remember a time when Hephzibah used the hoe. She was the only one who used the hoe to faithfully till the soil and keep out the weeds. The good condition of the yard was due to Tabitha's work. Each time she used the hoe, she reliably put the hoe away in the garden shed. This is why the hoe remained in excellent condition.

"I don't use the hoe," Hephzibah admitted. She meant to put the hoe away for Tabitha. "I use the shovel," she said and then she paused. "Actually, I don't use the shovel either." The shovel was becoming harder to use. The leverage no longer felt right. It made her arms feel heavy. The shovel handle was heavier than when she first bought it. "I use the hand trowel."

"Which you always put away," Tabitha observed. "We used to have more of them."

"We used to have four," Hephzibah answered. "Now we only have two." There was a hand cultivator and a metal hand trowel. Those were missing. She looked down at the garden hoe with regret.

"Just leave it," Tabitha replied. "That wasn't it." She held Ebony in his coffin and was eager to complete his burial.

"No, I suppose not," Hephzibah answered. "A hoe might make an open wound," Hephzibah contemplated.

Hephzibah wanted Ebony buried near the raspberries They approached the backyard. Hephzibah looked over at the garden shed. The door that was stuck shut yesterday was open about an inch. She felt braver in daylight with a shovel in her hand. Hephzibah reached over and pulled the door open. The door moved effortlessly on the rail. She peeked inside the shed. She looked right and then she looked left. The shed was vacant. No man in canvas tennis shoes. There was no sign anyone was here. Yet the rail the door slid on was clear. There was no sign of obstruction. There was no explanation of why the door was stuck shut yesterday and open one inch today. The rail was level. The door couldn't open by itself.

"Now why did you do that?" Tabitha asked. "You already have the shovel."

"Just checking," Hephzibah answered. She began to dig a hole to bury Ebony near the raspberry bushes.

New Year's Eve was a small affair that year. Hephzibah expected a friend to stay the night, but she hadn't arrived and hadn't called. Tabitha and Hephzibah worked hard to clean, so that the house would be ready if she decided to come and needed a place to stay.

"Whose toothbrush is this?" Hephzibah asked Tabitha. She was trying to clean the bathroom.

"The green one was Rachel's," Hephzibah answered. "I don't know about the purple one."

"The purple one was Rachel's," Hephzibah corrected. She had seen the purple toothbrush in the holder for some time now.

"No, Rachel had the green one," Tabitha insisted.

Hephzibah took the purple toothbrush out of the toothbrush holder. She placed the toothbrush in the automatic dishwasher on the sterilization cycle. When the cycle was done, the toothbrush was sterilized and dry. She almost used the toothbrush as a scrubber. Instead, she put the toothbrush back into the toothbrush holder to check what would happen.

Later that day, she ran her thumb across the toothbrush bristles. The toothbrush was wet again. The water on the bristles was cold. This verified the toothbrush was used. Instantly she got a piercing migraine headache. Stress is the state where your brain doesn't have enough information to process what is happening. Hephzibah told Tabitha, "I have a headache. I need to lay down for a while." It was the only thing that would help.

Hephzibah went to the garden shed to take another look at the red bag. A spider made the bag into a home and created an egg sack on the side. She took an electrical extension cord and the vacuum cleaner and cleaned up the bag. She grabbed up the lotions and vibrator and threw them in the garbage. She threw the white mosquito netting into the trash. She looked at the soldering equipment. Jerry was a welder, not someone who solders. She left that in the bag for now.

Hephzibah found the extra sleeping bag. Sometimes it was there. Sometimes, when she wanted to use it, it was missing. The sleeping bag looked vaguely familiar, but not for the reason she first thought. A California king satin seafoam green comforter was next to it. California king for a tall man. Satin which feels silky. Seafoam green to be calming. This pointed to someone. Someone who shouldn't be here.

Hephzibah contacted police dispatch. Dispatch contacted the patrol officer with Code 647e Illegal Squatting, which says "Who lodges in any building, structure, vehicle, or place, whether public or private, without the permission of the owner or person entitled to the possession or in control of it." That code doesn't fully describe the situation. That description only hits an exterior slice of what is going on. The owner of that seafoam green comforter was dangerous.

Hephzibah worried, "The bag of lotions of different types, fragrances, and flavors would originate from various sources. This was a set up. As if I would commit murder to steal. Murdering to steal their bottle of lotion. Murder for petty theft. This is what people were to think of me."

The red overnight bag filled with lotions, an anal sex vibrator, Jerry's library card, soldering tools, anti-depressant medication, black plastic supports, a business card from probation services, and a magnifying flashlight. At the bottom of the overnight bag were two solid bronze trophies from 1952 and 1954 and a brass handbell. A key with a black rubber top, a garage door lock jammed with a key, and a small rock fell to the bottom of the bag. Memories and pieces started to fall together.

The 1952 and 1954 solid brass trophies from Jerry's apartment. There were the black supports that acted as Jerry's left arm. Jerry said he would never part with these. The magnifier might be one Jerry used to read. She was framed for stealing and framed for murder.

Hephzibah contacted the apartments where Jerry lived, and they could not provide any information due to confidentiality. She contacted Jerry's son who said, "I haven't had contact with my father for six to eight years. I'm not sure how long." That is how long Jerry has been missing.

The lieutenant came by and surveyed the house. He found two places on the west side where plant life was growing out of the crawl space. These locations were six feet from the corner of the house. "There is something threatening the foundation right here," he said.

"The tree roots?" Hephzibah asked, glancing back at the cherry tree.

He looked at the cherry tree, shook his head, and said, "No." He pointed at the extension pad and said, "Something right here. Plants need water to survive." The soil below a house is covered with rocks or a plastic vapor barrier.

"There wasn't anything growing here when I bought the place," Hephzibah said.

The lieutenant said in alarm, "Something happened."

When Hephzibah was asked to write a story, she planned to add more from a book on Taoism. The book on Tao was a book that was given to her many years ago. But it was missing from the dining room bookshelf. It was nowhere to be found. This was her first suspicion about the identity of the intruder.

Hephzibah mother relayed a conversation:

"Why didn't you tell me your parents left their house to you?" Hephzibah's mother asked Daniel.

"I didn't want to bother you with it," Daniel told her.

"Bother me with it!" Hephzibah's mother complained, "The house needed repair. It has some foundation problems."

"It didn't when his parents bought it," Hephzibah answered.

"His parents never met someone who brought home such horrible smells. Finally, they confined him to his room and that took care of it," Hephzibah's mother explained. "Then when it was just his mom, he was back at it again. There was nothing she could do to stop him. She couldn't have guests over. And she couldn't receive the medical treatment she needed." Hospice couldn't come to the house.

"Probably because of the smell," Hephzibah said.

In July 2022, Henco plumbing came to update the piping. The plumber came out of the crawl space and said, "Someone has spent a lot of time digging in the crawl space and the ants have really found something to eat!" He looked at Hephzibah's confused expression, "I thought you already knew about it."

In June 2023, the foundation estimator with Terrafirma silently gave Hephzibah a serious look. The estimator hesitantly passed a picture to Hephzibah of what he found under the house. She braced herself for the sight of a dead body. She was prepared for everything, except this. She saw the white rib cage lying against the black vapor barrier. The shape of the attached skull, eye sockets, and teeth. It was a picture of a skeleton.

A scream caught in her throat. The only thing that stopped it was guilt. How could she endanger Jerry like this? Her worst fears were about to be confirmed. She moved her gaze to the face. "Was it Jerry?" she wondered.

She studied the skeleton for any clues. She took a closer look at the shape of the skull. The skull looked rodent-like. There was no size dimension. Was it a rabbit? The skulls are the same. She moved her gaze to the base of the skeleton. No, it had a long thin tail. It was a rat; the skeleton was a brown rat. These wandered along the railroad track line. It was not Jerry. Her cat completed his mission. An invading brown rat was dead. She shook her head at herself and handed the picture back to the estimator.

"Were there any live rats down there?" Hephzibah asked.

The second estimator joked, "If there was, he would run out of there screaming like a little girl." The first estimator laughed. There was also debris from the dryer vent.

The estimator continued, "There is sign of water intrusion. The building code requires a 10-12" overlap in the vapor barrier. The earth is exposed and there is a depression. This is indication of water intrusion."

Hephzibah translated the news from the estimator. The lack of overlap in the vapor barrier could be a gravesite. The exposed earth could be a digging spot. The depression, the location of a dead decomposed body. She was not optimistic.

Below the house, Terrafirma found old piping from the repair of the main line back in October 2016. There was a place where the vapor barrier should overlap by twelve inches. Instead, there were breaks in overlap of the vapor barrier and a depression in the soil there. There were rips in the vapor barrier along the edge. There were no ants. Oddly, there was a piece of cast iron pipe in the crawl space. There was no explanation for the cast iron pipe.

"Why was there a cast iron pipe in the crawl space?" Hephzibah wondered. "Did Daniel Bondehagen put it down there to frame me for murder?" They might follow the Clues and guess, "Miss Scarlet in the Hall with a Lead Pipe." Was that the conclusion people were supposed to come to? Hephzibah pondered, "Daniel is so careful; he washes the shovel in hot, soapy water. Apparently, I'm so careless; I left the murder weapon right next to the grave. And I use cast iron as if I'm Rapunzel in the Disney movie Tangled."

Daniel's best friend was Gary Ridgway, the Green River Killer. Over nearly 40 years, Daniel has more serial kills than Ridgway and Ted Bundy combined. He is now the most prolific serial killer in American history, a profile in the shadows. Hephzibah had a protection order against him, but it barely helped.

In July 2023, Hazel Dell Appliance came out to repair the dryer vent. The repairman said, "The dryer vent was knocked loose." He added, "Maybe when they were doing work down there."

Tabitha said, "None of the ghosts are Jerry." This is true. But that introduces another topic. "But don't you think Jerry would find a way to contact us if he was here?" Tabitha asked. It might be a valid point. There was still no explanation for the raised floorboard in the hallway. Or the mud streaks across the kitchen floor.

# The Red Bag

There was an unlikely friendship between Navid and Hephzibah. Navid was a Shiite Muslim. They worked together for four years. When Hephzibah conducted audits, she used Navid as an example of someone who does his job well.

Navid knew Hephzibah tried to understand the clues at her house. He followed the case closely and had a theory. He asked her about the shovel. "Is there a place outside where he could soak a shovel in hot, soapy water?"

Hephzibah said, "There is an extra cat litter box. But that isn't large enough." There was nothing else outside.

Navid answered, "That's what I thought. He is bringing the dirty shovel inside."

Hephzibah said, "He is washing the shovel in the bathtub. That explains the dirt chunks and leaves." It wasn't Tabitha making that mess.

Navid nodded and pointed out. "He has to put the shovel down to open the door."

Hephzibah gasped, "Quietly. He must have put the shovel down gently so he could open the door without making much noise."

Daniel no longer purchased a new shovel every other week, as he did at the hardware store on West James Street in Kent. Instead, he soaked the shovel in hot, soapy water, using the dish soap from Hephzibah's kitchen. That is why the dish soap was running low without use. This is why there were leaves, stems, and chunks of dirt in the bathtub. And this is why the shovel handle was swollen and smooth, the paint was gone, and the glue between the plywood layers dissolved.

Hephzibah was emotionally torn over the war in Israel. Hephzibah wrote in her diary:

"October 7, 2023: Hamas attacked Israel this morning. I am so numb; I can't feel anything. I expected to spring into action. All I can do is watch. Israel isn't allowed to use the weapon I helped design, even though it is only for defense. The USA spent an enormous amount of money trying to reinvent the wheel. I'm convinced whatever weapon they come up with to replace it won't be nearly as good. It won't be as exact or as fast. I assume any other effort I make will be squashed as well. I'm spent out."

With Hephzibah's contribution to the design in Israel, the Iron Dome stopped 2,000 out of 2,000 missiles fired from Gaza. There were no hits. But now the U.S. would not allow Israel to use the defense weapon.

The United States asked Israel how the Iron Dome worked. Israel responded, "It is one projectile hitting another projective."

Jerry an area manager explained, "The US attempted to use artificial intelligence (AI) to improve the reliability of Israel's Iron Dome. AI proved to be hazardous. The aims became worse, not better. After spending an exorbitant amount of money, the project was stopped."

Muslims at Hephzibah's work felt comfortable with her. It was a situation of mutual respect, and it was kept in a delicate balance. But Hephzibah could not overlook the violence of Hamas against the Jews.

Rai, an operations manager at Hephzibah's work who was born in Dubai, told her, "We can't speak against Hamas. It shows bias against Muslims."

Navid, her coworker, came to Hephzibah's side and defended her. He said to Rai, "Muslims don't advocate violence," and, "Don't judge us by Hamas." Navid didn't want people speaking for Muslims who did not understand that Islam is a peaceful religion.

Hephzibah agreed there was nothing wrong with the Palestinians living in the region and the Jews who purchased the land were trying to run them out. The Palestinians developed the land. It would be similar to Great Britain selling Manhattan Island, after giving it up in the war of 1776.

Navid wants me to add, "It would be similar to Great Britain selling Manhattan Island <u>to a foreign country</u>." This is the Palestinian viewpoint and why they view the government as corrupt.

When Israel purchased land for cities from Great Britain, they assumed the land between the cities would remain rural and part of the same country, not become part of a foreign country. This difference of viewpoints is the reason for the conflict.

Rai said, "The Palestinians were there first."

Hephzibah said, "Real estate records go back a long way. If you check, you'd be surprised."

Rai said, "Palestinians are descendants of Ishmael."

Hephzibah disagreed. She didn't have a chance to explain. But Abraham had seven sons, not two. The Palestinians have a prouder heritage than a line to a slave boy. And a line to Ishmael has never been found.

Despite Navid's best efforts to help Hephzibah, after the disagreement with Rai, she was released from employment.

This gave Hephzibah and the lieutenant extra time on their hands. The lieutenant met with Hephzibah.

Previously The Iron Dome was reported to be 90% effective. Hephzibah explained their math error. She explained the math to the lieutenant, "Calculating it any other way would produce the wrong answer." She smiled, "Thank you for asking. Usually, when I say I know how Israel's Iron Dome works, they assume I'm theorizing and then I'm dismissed."

The lieutenant explained, "The United States requested the information from Israel, and they didn't provide it. That's the problem."

"They may not have understood how it worked. They took my information and didn't involve me again in the project," Hephzibah explained.

Hephzibah and the lieutenant watched a movie with their favorite actors, but the plot was slow. She asked the lieutenant, "Can a rock be thrown and look like a pellet gun?" She had a new idea about the hole in her window.

He considered the double panes and the broken shards of glass lying between them. "I think it is significant that the bullet did not go through both panes of glass," the lieutenant commented. The pellet gun needed to be fired from a distance, but the neighbor's house was too close for that distance to be possible.

In the red bag, a rock carved into the shape of a pellet lay at the bottom against the black lining. "He wasn't expecting you to put that together. He didn't think you were smart enough. The bullet holes were a diversion. He knew you wouldn't think of him. You knew he never used a gun."

"It must be triggering to see the bullet hole each time you pass by your window." The lieutenant said, "The salesperson must have seen that. He sold you two other windows instead to give you something else to look at." The lieutenant had PTSD from when his military truck was hit by a grenade during the war. He knew about triggers.

The seafoam green satin comforter was a definite sign that Daniel was there. She had a protection order against him. A restraining order would be better, but a protection order was what the county judge approved. Hephzibah said, "When I saw the magnifying flashlight, I assumed Jerry used it to read." Then Hephzibah remembered, "Jerry said he was blessed with good eyesight, a gift from his mother." As she held the flashlight, her mind flashed back into the past.

[I looked down at the magnifier with caution. I thought back to when we lived in Kent, next to the Meeker Street Bridge. This was shortly before the five dead bodies were found.

"I use this magnifier while digging at night," Daniel explained to me with a laugh.

"You mean while camping?" I asked Daniel.

"No," Daniel replied. He didn't want to continue the conversation. I asked too many questions.

"When we were in Kent, he used the magnifier to redirect the beam of the flashlight." I realized, "This would minimize detection."

It was strange to hold it in my hands. "I was never allowed to touch it." He mumbled about it being harder to clean. I hadn't thought about it before.

"Maybe it was because the tool was too valuable, or maybe he didn't want fingerprints."

*\*\*Daniel Bondehagen will be explained in the next sections. \*\*]*

"That is why my flashlights kept dying," Hephzibah said with a gasp. "I thought they were defective. It was maddening. I kept buying more batteries and finally gave up."

In the bottom of the red overnight bag was a brass handbell and a key. What were they doing there?

Hephzibah appreciated Navid's suggestion about the shovel. It explained how the shovel was weathered by hot, soapy water. But the streaks were too short and too narrow for a dead body, and a different shape than what a shovel would make.

Daniel learned to do a finishing touch after sweeping when he worked in janitorial services at Seattle Pacific University. These weren't jobs he kept for long. He procrastinated too badly to keep him on the janitorial staff. He finished sweeping by laying the broom next to the door and sweeping outwards with two strokes. That is what caused the mud streaks.

Hephzibah was so worried Daniel caused mud streaks by dragging dead bodies across the kitchen floor, she didn't think about the muddy broom. A boy scout did a derelict boat removal project and found 14 abandoned boats down by the river. Hephzibah remembered the men at the marina and her trip down to the water with Alfredo and the scattered dirt. "I think I know where Daniel was digging," she said to the authorities.

During her time of grief, she wrote this ballad:

*Antique cars, county fairs, and hickory smoked brown trout*
*Shrimp gumbo, black pepper, Fat Tire and stout*
*I miss you, Jerry. The lights have gone out.*
*You wore the red jacket that I found.*
*Maybe if I had been there, you'd still be around.*
*You had one hand to zip your jacket.*
*Yet your smiles and humor never lacked.*
*Antique cars, county fairs, and hickory smoked brown trout*
*Shrimp gumbo, black pepper, Fat Tire and stout*
*I miss you, Jerry. The lights have gone out.*
*Having one arm never held you down.*
*Maybe if I had been there, you'd still be around.*
*I didn't look for the life jacket.*
*He took it with him in a white sack.*
*Antique cars, county fairs, and hickory smoked brown trout*
*Shrimp gumbo, black pepper, Fat Tire and stout*
*I miss you, Jerry. The lights have gone out.*
*I wouldn't be surprised if you were drowned.*
*Maybe if I had been there, you'd still be around.*
*Library card in place of the jacket*
*Library card had your name, oh frack!*
*Antique cars, county fairs, and hickory smoked brown trout*
*Shrimp gumbo, black pepper, Fat Tire and stout*
*I miss you, Jerry. The lights have gone out.*
*You wore the red jacket that I found.*
*Maybe if I hadn't been there, you'd still be around.*

Rachel's trip to Colorado ended. And her final trip to Colorado was fruitful in many ways. She graduated with a science degree. She wanted to do forensics. The Colorado Attorney General's Office decided to step in and assist where the local authorities had not. The Colorado AG was "offended" at how many of America's most prolific serial killers came from Washington state. This created a dramatic turn of events.

Previously the university objected to Hephzibah's request to talk with her math professor. Her request to talk with the professor was to warn the professor about a vagrant who was at his house. The vagrant at the professor's house stole from his savings account. It was easier to see the vagrant at his house instead of the vagrant at her own. She admitted the vagrant at her house was worse.

The math professor contacted Hephzibah through Messenger. He wanted to know if she was interested in getting together with him. He was fired from the university after she left, and he accepted employment elsewhere. He said he hadn't reported her as stalking him. He received a telephone call that Hephzibah was stalking him. The reporter was an anonymous third party.

Hephzibah declined the professor's invitation. After everything she went through, she was cautious.

Was Daniel the anonymous third-party reporter? It would fit some of the clues.

The state pressed charges against the intermediary who brought the case before the university's Student Conduct Board. The state attorney general said, "She should have verified her witnesses, at the very least." The state attorney general noted that Hephzibah had a solid alibi. When the professor was told he was stalked, she was across town giving Rachel a ride to another college.

This moved the sequence of events with the university's Student Conduct Board closer to a resolution. Originally the state assumed Hephzibah was not allowed to use her college degree, and their assumption was wrong. The state made a policy to check before prohibiting a graduate from using their degree.

The U.S. military facilitated another resolution. The lieutenant relayed Hephzibah's calculations and software information to the U.S. military. Later Israel's Iron Dome stopped 5,000 out of 5,000 missiles fired at Israel from Iran. There was not a single hit, zero. After failing to save this one man's life, it was reassuring to save many others.

# The Padded Jacket

In the winter of 1993, Bill Roberts was a security guard for the Fraternal Order of Eagles. His work shift started at dinner time and went until the wee hours of the morning.

One night, while working, Bill heard a gunshot. Boom. Then he heard 3 shots in succession. Boom, boom, boom. This was too close to his work. Only a block and a half away, a man had stolen a gun, knocked the gun's owner to the ground, and shot him.

That didn't end the fight. The man who lay on the ground grabbed back his gun and fired three times at the thief as he ran away. The gun owner was put on trial for excessive force. Bill was called in for jury duty. He let them know he knew about the incident, so he was excluded from the jury.

Later that month, Bill came home to tell me, "A teenage girl was at a convenience store hold up."

"Yes, I know," I answered. "I'm the teenage girl." I was older, but I passed as a teenager. I was wearing a white lace shirt, faded blue jeans, and tennis shoes.

"Whoa," Bill said in a breathy voice. Bill sat down on the sofa while I told him about my adventure. He was all ears. He leaned forward, his elbows rested on his knees, and his hands were folded.

I explained to Bill, "I decided to stop at the convenience store to see if they had good magazines. There was a young man behind the cashier's counter with his arms held downward. I peeked around, expecting the magazines to be near there. From this view, I could see the young man was holding a rifle. The barrel of the rifle was pressed hard against the right cheek of a police officer who was lying on his stomach on the floor behind the counter."

I told Bill, "When I first saw the young man, I thought he was the cashier. I almost asked him for assistance in locating their magazines. I stopped short."

Bill asked me questions, but I didn't know how the police officer ended up on the floor. And I didn't think to look for employees. I couldn't take my eyes off the gun. I told Bill what I knew.

The building was warm and humid. It smelled of cheese pizza and pretzels. The air was stagnant. With each breath, my lace shirt stuck to my chest. The only thing I could hear was the sound of my own breath and the faint sound of traffic passing by. The open front door was the primary ventilation. But flies hadn't found the entry. The floor was swept, but not mopped. Shoulder height white shelves made parallel lines around the room.

The police officer lay face down on the floor behind the counter. His face was distorted by the rifle barrel. The gums above his teeth were exposed as the gunman pressed down hard. The police officer began to pray for help. He only stopped praying to glance up at me.

One small noise escaped my mouth when I saw the police officer on the floor. My hands went up in a surrender position and my feet became glued to the floor. I didn't move a muscle.

A teenage boy was near the back bending over the bags of chips and made the selection of a green bag. He started to walk up to the cash register. He stopped six feet from the counter. He looked at me and used sign language. "Call 911?" he asked, mouthing the words.

I gave a quick nod and then looked back at the scene. The young man with the rifle hadn't noticed the interaction.

The teenage boy had a cell phone. He went outside and dialed. He waited in the front of the store for the police. While he waited, he opened his potato chips and began to munch.

I was thankful he went outside to use his phone. It seemed like more teenagers had cell phones than adults back then. The teenage boy hadn't paid for the chips, I didn't care at that point. The cash register was clearly closed.

A short while later three police cars pulled silently into the parking lot. The young man who was eating potato chips motioned for the police officers to enter. I was confident this was about to go bad. The only ending I could see was the young man shooting the police officer in the face, shooting me in the chest, and then shooting each of the police officers as they walked into the convenience store. The rifle probably didn't hold enough bullets for that scenario, but I didn't know that. All I knew was that I would take the second bullet. I gasped. The police officer noticed my worried expression when I glanced back at the front door.

I looked on the opposite side of the young man. There was a window displaying a park. A man was flying a kite with his son. Some children were riding bicycles. Mothers were watching their children play in the playground. They seemed happy.

I looked back at the young man with the rifle. He seemed troubled. In a comforting tone, I said, "I don't think you woke up this morning intending to be here. I think something went wrong today."

The young man nodded. His facial expression turned to sadness.

"Look out that window," I said. I nodded towards the park. "That could be you flying a kite or riding a bicycle." I looked out the window at the park, leading the young man's gaze. The young man glanced out the window at all the engaged faces. It was a picture you might see painted by Norman Rockwell. The young man's facial expression changed to one of hope and longing. For a second, he paused.

The police officer hadn't been working out. But he was covered in sweat. He looked up at the young man and watched his gaze. The police officer knew something was coming, but he didn't know what. He needed to protect me. Either way, he wanted that gun.

I didn't see how the police officer did it. I heard a shuffle. I closed my eyes tight. I made my body as narrow as possible to avoid a gunshot. I put my hands higher into the air and cringed. If I was able to evaporate in space, I would do it. When I opened my eyes again, the police officer had the rifle at the young man's back.

The police officer was pressing down hard with the rifle to restrain the young man. He prepared to aim the gun to shoot in one fluid motion. He looked up at the front door and paused. His police partner was standing there with a beaming smile. The other police officers filled the front door. Some police officers stood in the doorway, glanced behind them at the group, and then moved forward to collect suspects.

"I walk in the door just in time to see you restraining the man with his own gun," the police partner praised. He put handcuffs on the young man and police officers paired up to walk him to the police car.

A female police officer asked, "Should I take her in too?" She was referring to me.

The police officer shook his head.

"Well, I don't know," the female police officer said. "She is just standing there."

"You didn't see the scene when we first walked in," the partner responded.

Instead of going along with his police comrades, the police officer leaned his back against the counter next to where I stood. "How did you know he wasn't going to shoot you?" he asked.

"I didn't move my feet," I answered. "I kept them glued to the floor. Even now." I looked down at my feet and forced myself to lift a foot off the floor.

"I was praying for someone to come help me," the police officer said. "I thought you would call the police. But you didn't. You stayed with me."

"The teenage boy buying chips called the police," I answered.

"I didn't see that," the police officer said.

"He was buying chips in the back. I signaled for him to make the call," I answered.

"I'll keep your name out of the police report," the police officer offered. With that, he left to join his group. I walked home.

I was standing the whole time I told the story to Bill. Now that I was done, I sat down. It was my first chance to relax since the event occurred. I had a chance for my adventure; now Bill would have his.

Two rival gangs were in the city. One gang wore red, while the other gang wore blue. Each gang originated from a prison family in California. Men who were released from prison in the same year had children who intermarried. One evening there was a shooting at Davis High School. Bill planned for our children to attend school. This was too close to home, and this was too close to his work. The two incidents together pushed Bill into action.

Bill changed his clothes several times before approaching the gangs. He put on blue jeans but worried about looking partial to blue. He put on white tennis shoes and then cursed taking them off again because of the blue Nike swish on the side. After each clothing choice, he stopped to look in the full-length mirror. He was a 1970's man for clothing style, so he settled on a brown velour jogging suit with black tennis shoes.

Bill arranged a face-to-face meeting with the rival gang leaders. He had to approach contacts he knew. This drew on his previous life. The rival gang leaders came to the negotiation. Bill was surprised to find out who they were. From his perspective, the leaders seemed to be smaller players. The leader of the Blue gang was a middleman drug dealer. The leader of the Red gang ran a meth manufacturing lab.

Each group was allowed to bring anyone they wanted. The next in command was there as well, always on the ready to take over. That status could change at any moment. There was a succession that ensured the gang's survival, and all needed to be informed. Nothing was more important than making sure the gang continued. The second, third, fourth, fifth, sixth, seventh, eighth, ninth, tenth and eleventh in line came to the meeting. The eleventh in line of the blue gang was a little guy. They knew no one would shoot a child.

Bill moderated the meeting. He noticed that some of the Red gang wore blue jeans, and jeans could have been a clothing choice. The gangs listened to his request for a neutral zone. His neutral brown jogging suit helped them see this as a possibility, and the goal was something they all wanted to achieve.

The whole time he knew their guns were pointed at him. He could see the shape of a gun in the hand pocket of their jackets. It was very uncomfortable. The skin on the back of his neck was crawling.

[Years later the brown velour jacket was repurposed into a bear costume for Halloween. The brown jogging pants never surfaced again. "I was so frightened, I shit my pants," Bill confessed.]

In the end, the boundaries of the drug war were drawn. Davis High School was neutral territory. This territory included his work and our house. This was a great success. The city police took credit for his accomplishment, even though they had nothing to do with it. This makes the problem that happened next more calculated.

My parents gave Bill a new jacket. It was a nice jacket, red and black plaid, padded with insulation for cold winter nights. He was proud to own it. One evening when Bill went to work, he hung his new padded jacket on the coat rack inside the front double doors.

A volunteer was monitoring the door to ensure only members passed through. She gave Bill a nod of approval.

Then Bill turned to the right to walk the hallway towards the main room.

Just before Bill rounded the corner, another man walked through the double doors. He glanced to the right over at Bill, who had his back to him. Then he took the new jacket off the coat rack, put it on, and walked out of the building. That was the last day Bill saw his jacket. He only had it for a week.

For decades after, my parents complained about Bill "losing" the jacket and not taking care of his things. "You can't even buy him something nice," my mother complained.

The bar at Bill's work sold pull tabs. When changing out a new game, the old game was sacked, secured, and put in the dumpster. A man pulled the old game out of the dumpster and turned the pull tabs in for money. "I'll never forget that face," Bill said.

A short while later, an old friend went to visit my father. They went for a walk outside, and he grabbed his jacket. He was wearing the same red padded jacket. My father thought he must have purchased the same jacket for both men. It was too bad that Bill didn't take care of his jacket as well as this man did. His jacket looked as good as new.

My mother corrected him, "You didn't buy jackets for both."

"But he had one," my father protested. "And it was the same jacket. Purchasing the same jacket for both men is the only explanation."

But it wasn't the only explanation. Daniel Bondehagen was the "old friend" of my father. Daniel, who stole the jacket was praised while Bill, whose jacket was stolen was criticized. Daniel stole Bill's jacket before Jerry Taylor saw it.

**My acknowledgment** to editor Rebecca Henderson, author of *Serving with Significance* and *Thoughts on Turning Sixty-Five,* for editing *The Murder of Jerry Taylor* and *The Padded Jacket.*

The next three sections are from my life near Meeker Street Bridge in Kent, Washington when the five bodies were buried there.

# Blow Up Dolls

## Searching the Closets for Blow Up Dolls

It was January 1984. I rented a room in a three-story house east of the Seattle Pacific University campus in north Queen Anne. The outside of the building had dark gray cedar shake siding. The front of the house was elevated with stairs to a full front porch. The main floor held a large living room, kitchen, dining area, and bathroom. The living room had a dark green carpet. The living room had a musty "old people" smell, even though everyone who lived in the house was young.

The house was built on a downhill slope. The room I rented was in the basement on the east side of the house. The basement had a faint moldy smell. Daniel showed me around the room. "This door leads to a closet," Daniel said. He faced the door, placed his right hand on the doorknob, and tried the knob to show it didn't move. "The door is locked, see. I promised the landlord I wouldn't open the closet."

I sat on the top bunk bed with my legs dangling over the edge and nodded. I paid the rent for the apartment. I rented it for Daniel to live in while he was dealing with depression and getting back on his feet. Daniel stayed there while he pulled himself together emotionally and financially. It was meant to be a temporary measure. I was certain he could work if given a chance.

I hadn't expected to move in. It was unfortunate circumstances that led me to need a place to stay. Taking care of an elderly woman with brain cancer didn't last long. And I unexpectedly needed to leave. I worked nine days straight and couldn't go out for a two-hour movie. Daniel wanted me to come with him and his friends. It would be a double date. I had it. I quit. In Viola's words, "It didn't pan out."

February 1984, Daniel and I goofed around. We hadn't had sexual intercourse. We preferred to wait until marriage. But we slept together in the same room. "You are the first live woman I've slept with," Daniel said. He looked at my face and gave a solemn nod. Daniel meant this as a compliment. But his statement didn't seem quite right. Why was there an emphasis on the word "live"? I asked a male tenant who rented a room on the main floor what Daniel might have meant.

The housemate was downstairs dropping off his laundry. "The women he sleeps with are usually dead?" he asked.

"I think he is referring to pornography," I replied with uncertainty.

"Blow up dolls?" the housemate asked with a laugh. He laughed, "You'd better check the closets for blow-up dolls." He gave a humorous side glance as he passed through the hallway. Then we walked away, back up the stairs to his room. He shook his head and continued to chuckle.

I didn't know what blow-up dolls were. I assumed he was referring to dolls that explode. I shuddered. I waited to gather my courage. I carefully opened each of the closet doors, taking care to be gentle in case the doll was triggered by movement like a hand grenade. The last closet door I tried was the door for the closet Daniel promised the landlord he would never open.

When I opened the door, it wasn't a closet at all. It was a door to the outside. There was a stepping stone path that led to the front sidewalk. The stepping stones were round. The stones were made of cement and decorative rock. The stones were sparsely surrounded by mowed grass.

Rose bushes that lost their leaves stood waiting for winter to complete. They weren't in the best of care, but someone pruned them. I waited until Daniel was home to ask him about the door to the outside. "I'm sorry I opened this closet door," I apologetically explained. "I noticed the door isn't a closet. It leads to the outside."

Daniel paused and was silent. He stared at the closed door and then admitted, "I knew about the door to the outside, but I would prefer if you use the main door." He said something about the lock. Then he added, "We can leave by this side door," Daniel explained, "But let's always return by the main entrance. So, that the other tenants see when we return." He looked at me to make sure I agreed.

I didn't understand the reasoning, but I agreed to this rule. Daniel went upstairs. When he came back downstairs to the room, he was cross at me for asking the other tenant about what he said. "Don't tell the other tenants what I say to you," Daniel complained, "I had to lie to him."

My legs dangled over the edge of the bed and my ankles were crossed. My back was hunched over, and my head was down. I was buried in my textbook. I struggled to memorize the Latin words. I was sitting on the upper bunk bed studying my anatomy and physiology book. We were learning the names of the bones in the human body.

"I didn't think it," Daniel said in awe after he walked through the apartment door. The words on the page blurred. I barely looked up other than a glance to verify who was talking. "Because we are in the basement," he finished his sentence. "But there is a crawl space. There is plenty of room under there."

I expected his next line to invite me to come and see. I was aggravated at the interruption to my studies. Instead of inviting me, he disappeared again. This time he was gone for a while. This met my needs, so it didn't concern me. It was peaceful with him gone for a couple hours. It gave me a chance to read. Later in the night, when I was mostly asleep, I saw Daniel slide out the side door. I heard him but pretended to be asleep.

When Daniel came back, he used the same side door, violating his own rule. He slowly rotated to close the side door. He walked straight through the room. He was hunched over while crossing the room from the side door to the bedroom door. He was at nearly a 90-degree angle so that his torso was almost parallel with the floor.

I looked at his facial expression expecting to see nausea or pain. It was dark in the room, but I could see his eyes. The dim light in the room reflected off his eyes. He was pleasantly facing forward looking at the door in front of him. He didn't look to the side or to the floor. He exited the bedroom door towards the laundry room. But he didn't go into the laundry room. That would wake another tenant who shared the basement.

When Daniel returned, he ducked down to go into his bunk. I turn onto my side in my bunk to face the wall. Daniel became startled, stood back up, and stared at me for a long time. He was also loudly sniffing me. This was very uncomfortable. I tried to lay still and not move a muscle. Finally, he turned and climbed into his own bunk.

The next day I asked him, "Are you feeling nauseous?" I hoped to understand why he was hunched over.

"I'm fine," he answered with a soft smile. He told me, "I had to convince myself it was okay for you to move." He said this to explain why he was startled when I rolled over in bed.

I asked the tenant who shared the basement, "How did you sleep?"

"Fine," the tenant answered with a cheerful, well-rested demeanor.

The next day the smell was horrible. Daniel stood in the bedroom, perfectly still except for his eyes moving back and forth. He was breathing deeply in through his nose and out of his mouth. He was grateful for the smell, doing nothing to combat it, fascinated.

It stank. The smell is one I'll never forget. I sprayed Lysol to kill any bacteria that might be causing the smell. I sprayed it through the air. I used half a can.

Daniel stood and watched me spray the Lysol. He did not step in to help. Instead, he seemed fascinated by an accomplishment. His mouth was open as he avoided breathing through his nose. But he was smiling. "That's better," Daniel praised. "Hey, how does that work?" he asked.

I read the information on the front of the Lysol can and explained what that means.

Daniel nodded. I handed him the can of Lysol. He took the can and sprayed some more. Then he sprayed two cans of Lysol. The Lysol barely took the edge off the smell. The Lysol was so thick in the room.

The layer of Lysol in the air rose in the atmosphere. It hung over my bed in a cloud. The Lysol stuck to the back of my throat and made it hard to breathe. I pulled a blanket over my mouth, but it was little help. The chemicals were hurting the back of my throat. I lay on the top bunk coughing through the night. The back of my throat felt raw.

We moved out. I just wanted to move away from there. Kent was a safer community. But the problem followed me. After we moved out, the landlord refused my security deposit. I hadn't expected it. The landlord telephoned to complain to me. He said, "I had to air out the room for three days before I could rent the room out to someone else. The smell was not better after I spent three days airing out the room in the dead of winter."

"How did you air out the room?" I asked. This was a better idea than spraying two cans of Lysol.

"I opened up the side door and padded up the interior door," the landlord answered.

"Do you believe in ghosts?" Daniel asked. "If you pretend that you can't see them, they go away." He stopped. "See, just like that," he held his right hand up and he laughed. All I could think was that I was living with someone who was crazy.

## Friendly Advice About Cabbage

In April 1984, I had a battle with smell mitigation. I rented a studio apartment in Kent. There was a four-foot-tall half divider and a step between the living room and bedroom area. This gave the nice effect of a separate room. My apartment was near the Meeker Street bridge. I wasn't just in one of the apartments near the Meeker Street bridge. It horrifies me to realize this. I was in <u>the</u> apartment closest to the Meeker Street bridge. I allowed my boyfriend Daniel to move in with me while he was getting back on his feet financially. It seemed like a kind thing to do. He was a tall blonde man with blue eyes.

Daniel bragged he could sell anything. "My friends tell me I could sell snake oil," he said. He looked at me and smiled. "Do you want some snake oil?" he asked me. "It cures all ailments."

"No thanks," I responded. "I'm sure you would need it more than me." I was usually healthy. I ate the right food and exercised. Daniel was sick more often. If he had snake oil that cures ailments, he should use it on himself. This was my evidence that the potion didn't work.

"Hey, the conversation wasn't supposed to go like that," Daniel protested. He was annoyed that I didn't play along and didn't laugh at his joke. He didn't seem like a salesman. I didn't care for his pranks either.

I opened the windows and doors of the studio apartment to set the mood for spring cleaning. I was in the kitchen going through the cupboards and wiping down the glasses to make them sparkle. The dishwasher was whooshing water and suds to clean the service dishes, plates, cups, saucers, silverware, and utensils. There was a large pile of sorted laundry in the middle of the living room floor; warm wash whites separated from cold water darks. I was going through the apartment looking for more things to clean. A vinyl recorder was playing music in the living room.

My neighbor walked by in stride; his full profile was visible. He was short with black hair. His wife was tall, thin, and blonde. "Just a bit of friendly advice," he smiled as he turned his head to the left in my direction. "You can let many things go bad, but never cabbage."

"Thank you." I was in the kitchen preparing to clean the oven. I had the oven cleaner spray in my right hand, and I set it down on the kitchen counter. I opened the white refrigerator door. I squatted down low to pull the clear crisper compartment on the right forward. "The closest thing I have to cabbage is lettuce." I pulled the lettuce out of the produce bag and showed it to the passing neighbor.

He turned and faced me. He stopped, frozen in place. He said each word of the next sentence slowly, as if each word was its own story, "What else makes that smell?" He was staring with eyes open wide. He surveyed the apartment, taking in every aspect. His eyes settled on the two piles in the middle of the living room floor.

I followed the gaze of his eyes and explained, "I probably need to do the laundry." I looked around for what might smell. My cleaning shifted from "old dust" and streaks on the glasses to "smell mitigation." I explain, "That was my plan for the afternoon, but I'll start it now." I set aside the oven cleaning supplies. The mess inside the oven wasn't that bad and could wait for another day. I transitioned to taking up the laundry.

My neighbor's voice was suddenly raspy. "The clothes," my neighbors said quietly. "It's in the clothes," his voice was barely a whisper.

He mouthed the words, more than he said them. His eyes remained wide. He intently gazed down at the two piles of laundry.

"Those are his clothes," I answer the question he didn't say. His eyes took it in. He was facing completely forward.

"What were you talking about?" my boyfriend Daniel snapped. He had come up the stairs to enter the apartment and saw the neighbor talking to me.

"Laundry," I answered. I am used to talking to neighbors, getting to know them, and inviting them to events. I consider them to be people for lasting relationships. People I would catch up with later and find out how they are and what is new.

"Why were you talking about laundry?" he asked me. He stared down at the neighbor. The neighbor looked frightened and startled. Daniel closed all the windows and doors and closed the curtains. "Stop talking with the neighbors," he commanded. So much for being in the mood for spring cleaning! My social life took a hit. I didn't notice at the time. It was a gradual decline into social isolation.

Daniel brought home a kitten. It was a Russian blue he found in a bush. The kitten was hissing and spitting. Daniel named the kitten Nipper. Nipper liked to play with the neighbor's cat. Their cat was a calico.

One early morning Daniel brought home a thin clear plastic filled with blood as a special treat for the two cats. The thin plastic was like Saran wrap. The pool of red blood was in the center. It looked like he carried the wrap of blood to the apartment, because the blood hadn't spilled over. Wherever he found it, it had to be somewhere close by.

The neighbor pulled back the curtain and watched Daniel and the cats through the picture window. The cats didn't want to lick the blood.

"You know where that came from don't you," Daniel stated with disappointment. Daniel came into the apartment and demanded, "Don't feed him anything else until he's finished with that."

I walked out to the balcony to the cats and said, "You don't really want this do you?" I took the plastic and red blood and threw it in the trash. I fed the cats dry cat food.

The neighbor came out to chat with me. "What was the blood from?" he asked.

"Beef, I think. Some sort of red meat," I answered.

"Do you have red meat in the house," he asked.

"No, it's been a while since we've been able to afford meat," I answered. I wondered if he planned to give us meat.

"What else did you notice about the blood?" he asked.

"It was very red. Beef blood tends to turn purplish brown," I answered. "The blood had a faint sweet smell. There was no rancid odor, no odor of decomposition."

"Do you know why?" He asked. "That's because it was fresh," he answered his own question. "I've heard enough," he said and left.

Later Daniel came back. "What did you do with the blood?" he asked.

"I threw it in the garbage. Things like that attract flies and maggots," I answered. I learned that lesson feeding the pigs in our barn.

Daniel started to move at me and then stopped. "You don't know what I did to get that," he said. He took the white 13-gallon garbage bag with its one small item and put it in the apartment complex dumpster. He replaced the kitchen garbage liner.

Later the cat snuggled up to me on the bed. "After all that, the cat snuggles up to you," Daniel complained. He moved off the bed. The cat slipped under the bed. Daniel stood next to where I was lying, picked me up off the bed, and dropped me hard onto the floor.

The cat came out from under the bed to sniff what Daniel dropped and was surprised it was me. Nipper let me pet him and then slipped back under the bed for safety.

"I thought after I did that, the cat would have to snuggle with me," Daniel complained.

Later the neighbor said, "I know you don't want to, but you need to look down at what the cats are eating."

"I know what they are eating," I replied. "I toss the scraps my husband gives them into the garbage and give them cat food."

"Where is he getting the scraps?" the neighbor asked. Cows were grazing nearby, but there were no places that butcher.

Daniel and I walked down West James Street, past the cattle pasture, and continued going straight. I looked down. There was a depression in the dirt, six feet long. The depression was shaped like a deflated tire. A small puddle of clear rainwater innocently rested in the center.

The property was near Meeker Street Bridge. There were plans to sell the property to create a golf course. The contract was not yet complete. The dirt was an odd color of pale, grayish, brown. It was the same color as my grandmother's beef gravy but without the saucepan charred lumps. The texture of the dirt was smooth, like soft silk. The dirt looked odd. But it wasn't as odd as Daniel's reaction.

Daniel moved his top lip in position to plug his nostrils. This is something only swimmers can do. His mouth was open but plugged from the air with his bottom lip. "I let you go in too far," he said. His face was still. I turned to walk back home in silence.

# Nectarine Daquiri

Shortly after I rented a one-bedroom apartment. I stood on a dining chair and watered the hanging spider plants. Daniel said, "Rape them and kill them, but not necessarily in that order," he laughed. "How does that sound?" Before I had a chance to process the statement, he turned to leave.

I peeked from behind the plant and looked at the door, my right hand was positioned over the plant holding the watering can. The apartment door shut behind him with a soft click. Where was he going? All this effort to keep the place looking nice, and no one saw it.

Later Daniel decided we would throw a party. He invited friends to my apartment and asked me who I wanted to invite. I decided on Greg, a friend of his from the university, work study, and the church youth group.

My apartment had an open space in the wall between the kitchen and the living room. The kitchen had a double basin sink. Daniel decided this would be a great place to serve drinks. He tasked me with bartending. This wasn't something I'd done before, but I know how to mix ingredients together, I don't have the gift of hospitality, and it was nice to have a specific job that kept me busy. The best part is that the bartender stays sober and isn't expected to drink, which was perfect for me. I went to the library to research how to make the drinks and purchased the ingredients.

Daniel asked me if there was anything I needed. I tried to have at least two of every type of measure so that I could have one drying while the other was in use. I looked through the drawer in my kitchen. I told him I needed a measuring spoon for one teaspoon. Daniel said Greg would bring the measuring spoon. Each guest brought something.

I have no idea how many people attended the party. Greg was the only guest I knew. He attended Seattle Pacific University with Daniel. Greg and Daniel did work-study together at SPU in janitorial services. They both attended the Methodist church. Greg felt sorry for Daniel and knew he needed a friend. Greg was 5'10" and had a round face, light hair, and light blue eyes.

Instead of coming with a measuring spoon, Greg came with information from his mother that any teaspoon would work. I had a drawer full of teaspoons. So, this information sufficed.

A guest at the party objected to Greg staying without bringing anything. I didn't know the guest. I didn't know any of Daniel's invites. I felt I did Daniel a favor by inviting one of his friends. I thought he would return the favor and invite some of my friends. I approved for Greg to say. This was the first attempt the guests made to muscle Greg out of the party.

Greg was a master at Trivial Pursuit. At the party, no one agreed to be Greg's partner. I was pulled from the kitchen. We teamed up together. I answered most of the questions. Greg let me take center stage. The group selected the category of Entertainment for our final round. Entertainment was my weak area, but Greg's strong suit. We won the game.

One guest complained, "Next time we choose teams, let's not have someone in the kitchen."

Daniel told Greg to leave early, saying, "Your mother needs you for something."

Greg knew Daniel was lying. But he left early and told me he decided to stop being a friend to Daniel. "If he wants me to leave, he can just tell me to leave," Greg told me with exasperation. "My mother knew I was out for a couple of hours, and she was fine with it."

I thought it was unkind of the group to dismiss Greg and I apologized to him. The situation was evidence that my husband led a double life. The guests who seemed like extras, arriving because all were welcome, saw themselves as the true part of the group.

In addition to his college friends, Daniel invited his friend Gary Ridgway, who was later known as the Green River Killer. Gary arrived late after the Trivial Pursuit game was over. He grabbed a cold beer for most of the night. But near the end of the party, he decided to request a nectarine daiquiri. Daniel told Gary we couldn't fix that. Then he told Gary not to show me his face to me, only his profile. Daniel said, "Profiles are harder to identify." Gary peeked around the corner to request the drink.

No one ordered a nectarine daiquiri yet. I was pleased to give that one a try. I put the ingredients through the blender and poured the frozen contents into a glass. Gary tried his best to only show me his profile while tasting the drink. He mainly succeeded, but not completely. He complimented me on the flavor.

I hadn't watched the news at all. I didn't know the real reason Daniel asked to move from the studio to a one-bedroom apartment. I had no idea who Gary was, and I wouldn't for many years. "Oh, there were just a few of us," Daniel said about the party, "Planning what we are going to do." He sounded disappointed, "No, there won't be another party."

Daniel was leaving, "They call it 'six feet under' for a reason," he said. "All I need to do is reach up to see if it's taller than me." He laughs and walks out the door.

After we separated, at the domestic violence support group, I confessed, "The thing that I hate the most is I don't have a chance to sleep." The support group met in a house. We sat in a circle in the living room. The location was subject to change as necessary for our protection.

"He doesn't let you sleep?" the counselor asked.

"I have to pretend that I'm asleep and that keeps me awake," I answered.

"Why don't you just go to sleep?" the counselor asked.

"People toss and turn while they sleep. If I turn over to a different position, he'll check to see if I'm awake," I answered.

"He wants you to play dead?" the counselor asked.

"I don't know," I answered. I'm thinking of a cute little dog exposing his soft underbelly. "He threatens to put duct tape down the bed to keep me on my side."

The counselor asked me, "You don't have the gift of hospitality, but you gave him a place to stay?" Daniel convinced me I didn't have hospitality. It was gaslighting.

Later I took a head of cabbage and let it rot to check how it would smell. A rabbit ripped open the bag and ate the cabbage before the smell was bad enough to equal the smell of Daniel's laundry.

The neighbor who gave me the advice about rotting cabbage talked with the Kent Police Department. He found me at my one-bedroom apartment. "I talked with the police," he said. "They didn't want to release this. However, they found 3 sets of DNA samples on the victims. The DNA was from semen. The semen was post-mortem, along with post-mortem vaginal and rectal bruising."

## The Man Who Left to Buy Groceries

One day at our studio apartment in Kent, I sang a Barbara Streisand song, "Evergreen". I hoped Daniel would like it. I learned to sing it as a child. I expected him to look pleased. In its place, he had a look of derision.

Daniel looked over the vinyl Barbara Streisand album. Instead, he wanted me to sing a song I usually skipped, "Prisoner" the love theme song from "Eyes of Laura Mars." I obediently learned to sing the song.

Daniel was sitting on the floor in the living room. As I sang, he started to become rigid. He softly chuckled and rotated his head forward with a stiff smile. His eyes darted side to side, but his facial expression never changed or moved. It was as if his body had become a statue. Even without moving, the capillaries on his head started to swell. The bald portions of his crown slowly went from pink to red and started to bead with sweat.

This wasn't the reaction I expected. I stopped singing and just studied him. Why did he want me to sing the song? This wasn't a look of pleasure.

Daniel ran and huddled in the corner, slapping and beating himself hard on the head and periodically laughing manically. I tried to distract him. He ran after me fast, all arms and legs. To avoid injury, I let my body go limp. When my body landed on the floor, Daniel ran out the door. I lay on the floor trying to process what happened. The sun was setting. It was getting close to dinner time so I went into the kitchen and worked as quickly as I could to have the dinner food prepared on time.

When Daniel came home, he looked at the location where my body was when he left. Then he looked at me in the kitchen stirring dinner on the stovetop. Then he looked back again at the floor, trying to understand what happened. "I expected you would be lying on the floor when I got back," he explained. "I left to eat a sandwich while trying to figure out what to do."

Daniel had already eaten dinner on my meager budget. I was recuperating from his attack and cooking his meal. After he struck me to the floor, he rewarded himself with a meal out. I was furious. He was not even concerned about my injuries. I was trying to make ends meet and he was throwing curve balls to my finances. Daniel left again to do more thinking. I ate my dinner. I was too grieved to enjoy it. Is this the thanks I get for taking this man in? I put the leftovers in the refrigerator and then went out onto the front balcony.

My neighbor came out onto the shared front balcony to talk with her. "I heard slaps and a loud thud," the neighbor said. "Then he left."

"You saw him leave?" I asked. She wanted to understand more about Daniel's reaction. Perhaps the neighbor and his wife saw the expression on Daniel's face as he was going out the door.

"I heard him leave," the neighbor said. "I didn't know when he was coming back. So, I waited to check on you." He was frightened of Daniel and wanted to avoid a confrontation.

"He left to get himself a sandwich," I explained.

"He hit you like that and then went to make himself a sandwich?" the neighbor exclaimed. He was expecting Daniel to feel remorse and to call for medical help for me.

"He left to buy himself a sandwich," I corrected.

"Same thing!" the neighbor exclaimed.

"I didn't fight back. I let my body go limp." I gestured back to where I had been lying on the floor. I attempted to explain how I avoided injuries in the attack.

The neighbor cut off my sentence, "No," he said. "You need to fight back," he was insistent. "If he is going to hit you like that, you need to fight back." The neighbor didn't want to encounter Daniel. So, he told me to come out onto the front porch if it was safe to talk. I was accustomed to hiding my injuries. So, the idea of coming out onto the front porch was revolutionary.

Later the FBI explained that I needed to look for motive, opportunity, and one more thing, the tendency to commit harm. I realize now how much a motive for one person is not the same as a motive for another. Tendency plays a role in establishing a motive. Daniel didn't consider petty theft as a weak motive. He almost committed murder over an ink pen. Once Daniel committed murder because he didn't like the way a man crossed the street.

When we first moved to Kent, James Street had cows to the west and cows to the north. Both cow fields contained marshland. The land seemed unsuitable for building. I was thankful these areas would remain untouched. Over time, the cow fields were cleared. The marshland was restructured into manmade lakes and expense apartments were built around the lakes.

This incident was before the bulldozers altered the landscape. There were a few apartment complexes on the north side of the road, closer to the city. The apartments were a stretch past James Street, hiding behind a thick patch of trees. There was usually little traffic in this part of town. The only place of excitement was the convenience store on the corner. This day was an exception. Traffic re-routed to bypass congestion and pass through on the way to the freeway.

A father, mother, and son were crossing James Street in Kent near the old railroad crossing. The railroad tracks there were no longer used. The tracks created rough patches in the road. There was a crosswalk there. The pedestrians had the right of way. The mother was tall and thin with brown hair. The father was athletic and had darker hair. The son was stockier than his parents. The son was about ten years old. I'm guessing the age was ten, because of his looks and because he acted very embarrassed by his father.

The father stepped out into the crosswalk with his family close behind. There was no traffic in the right-hand lane. A car stopped in the left-hand lane to let them pass. They crossed the right-hand lane and stepped out in front of the car that stopped. Then the family waited for the cars in the opposite direction to yield. The father held out his left arm like a fly wing to gesture for the rest of the family to stay back and wait.

The driver of the car in the left-hand lane became impatient. He put out both hands palm up alongside his steering wheel, raised his eyebrows, and leaned his head forward with wide eyes to indicate, "Aren't you going to move?"

The father of the family looked at the driver and then back at the oncoming traffic. It was a brief acknowledgment.

Annoyed, the driver shook his head. His face started to turn red as his expression turned into a scowl. When there was no change in the situation, the driver put his car in reverse. He drove in reverse just long enough to pull forward. Then he passed the family by driving in the right-hand lane across the crosswalk.

The ten-year-old son looked at the expression of the angry driver. He looked over at his father who continued to hold him back with an outstretched arm. The son dropped his jaw and took a sudden inhale. Then he put his left hand over his face in embarrassment and angled his face toward the right. The muscles in his face tensed. He no longer looked at the drivers.

"That's the funniest thing I ever saw," Daniel commented, as I drove down East James Street. I approached the railroad crossing slowly in the left-hand lane. A car passed me in the right-hand lane and swiftly passed the family standing in the crosswalk. The speed limit was 25 miles per hour. The car passed me at about 35.

The family was startled by the passing car and then the parents looked to see that they had no protection. They were standing in the middle of the road with cars approaching them. They grabbed their belongings tightly, held hands, and dashed across the road. Cars in the opposite lanes seemed surprised by the move and slammed on their brakes.

"Did the on-coming cars think they just wanted to stay standing in the road?" I asked, more to myself than to Daniel. I switched over to the right-hand lane to give the family extra space as I slowly passed the scene.

Daniel leaned forward in the passenger seat, rested his right hand on the dashboard, and turned his face to the left. "I think I know where they were heading," he said. He watched intently and nodded with certainty. His jaw was set. Then he settled back in the passenger seat. He looked forward. After we returned home, he said, "I'm going out." He was gone for about six hours.

When Daniel returned to the studio apartment, he settled down on the mustard yellow sofa. "He put up a fight, but I got him," Daniel boasted.

"He has a wife and children," I replied, confused at what he was saying.

"They are better off without him," Daniel replied in a definitive tone. He leaned forward with his elbows resting on his thighs in a catcher position. He looked over to the left towards the other apartment complex. "I drove his car down to the water. I found a girl to be in there with him. It didn't take long for one to come around." He sat up on the sofa and smiled. "The police can try to make sense of that." He looked at me with a startled and worried look, "What did you say?" he asked.

I was chopping vegetables and preparing dinner in the kitchen of my studio apartment. I looked at him confused. "I didn't say anything," I responded. I wasn't sure I wanted to know what he said. Asking him to explain would only alarm him and give me a headache.

"It wasn't you who was talking," Daniel realized. He looked around and left the apartment. I wondered if he was hearing voices now. This man is absolutely mad. He stepped out of the apartment and turned to the left. A while later he returned, "They were talking about something else," he said about the neighbors. Apparently, the walls in the apartment complex are too thin.

I didn't watch the news. So, I didn't know this at the time. When Gary Ridgway was captured by the police, they asked him about the man who left to buy groceries. The car was parked down by Meeker Street Bridge. They asked him about the girl. Ridgway answered, "I don't know anything about it." There was no further investigation.

This was after Daniel knocked me to the floor and thought I was dead. I didn't dare confront him. I hoped the neighbor overheard Daniel bragging. I didn't show it. Maybe if I was very lucky, I'd catch the neighbor out on the porch and discuss it with him. But it wasn't safe to even think those thoughts. If I thought about it, I'd gaze at the porch. Daniel would wonder why I gazed at the porch. The only safe course of action was to put the conversation out of my mind.

I relayed the story to my parents of the embarrassed 10-year-old boy. It was such a funny sight. Daniel told my parents there was no one standing in the road. I was just imagining things. My parents looked confused. Daniel looked straight at my parents and smiled, the same smile he gave when his mother complained to the family about him balancing the wine glasses on the edge of the shelf in the cupboard so that the glasses fall and break when the cupboard door is opened.

My neighbor from the studio apartment found me later with more friendly advice. "You should watch the movie 'Nuts' with Richard Dreyfuss and Barbara Streisand," he said. He gave no explanation.

1988 <u>Auto-bio-poem</u>

"Karen

Active, Playful, Protective, Listener

Who feels that all people deserve respect, no one should be hurt, that all people should be heard.

Who gives food to the hungry, entertainment to the bored, comfort to the lonely.

Who needs friendship, people, and conversation.

Who would like to see people give up their addictions, families live together in harmony, and countries give up their fears of each other.

Who fears the sound of a crash, the clash of a knife, and the cry of a woman or child."

# Hair Red Like a Flame

Daniel's next girlfriend didn't fare as well. It was 1987. She was a psychology major at Seattle Pacific University in her junior year. I think her name was Joan. It was too long ago to remember. Daniel said with a soft laugh, "She saw me in the student building at the university and took an interest in me." I short while later, he moved in. She had red hair like a flame. Daniel said, "She is so passionate."

Daniel took a job as a valet. There was a car owner who planned to leave the car for more than four hours. Daniel took it for a spin and brought it back with too much milage on the odometer and a horrible smell. It only takes once. Daniel was fired.

Joan deposited money into Daniel's checking account so that he could pay her rent. However, it wasn't his checking account; he was using my checking account. The court determined he was to close it. He kept writing checks on it, and he was bouncing checks around town. I couldn't buy food at my local grocery store without paying cash.

I asked my bank, "Can I close my account." I explained, "My ex-husband is bouncing checks." The bank teller allowed the closure. They sent me a check for the remainder. The amount was much less than what Daniel sponged off me. Daniel didn't contribute to the bills in his relationship with me or in his relationship with Joan. The amount left wasn't enough to cover anyone's rent.

Joan had to find more money to cover her rent. She called me at my work to complain. There was no reason to call me at work. She could easily have waited until I returned home. She claimed rights under some statute. This was a violation of the Protection Order I placed on Daniel. Daniel repeatedly used this statute as an excuse to have psychologists violate the Protection Order until his arrest.

Over the phone, I told Joan, "You aren't superwoman," I implored. "You need to get out," I warned her. There was nothing else I could do. The rest was up to her.

Daniel and a friend borrowed Joan's car. They didn't ask for her permission. Daniel's girlfriend tried to convince the police to stop Daniel from taking her car. Her reports had failed. She didn't know how long he was keeping the vehicle. He might have returned the vehicle and then borrowed it again, without her noticing. She didn't keep track. She didn't stay home awaiting his arrival. I always stayed home when he took my car, like a chained prisoner. The police required the vehicle to be gone for 24 hours before stepping in.

Daniel and the friend drove to Hood River to bury a body. At this point, they were trying to throw the police off their trail. On the way back, they were going down a hill. They took a turn at top speed. They totaled her car and had it towed. They requested for the car to become scrap metal.

Daniel couldn't afford to reimburse his girlfriend for the loss of her vehicle. The girlfriend told Daniel, "I want out." Daniel gave her a light green pill and a glass of half-and-half with crème de menthe. The half-and-half swirled in the crème de menthe until the color matched that of the light green pill. Daniel stood over her as she took the pill and drank. He wasn't taking "No" for an answer. The pill was heart medication, which is lethal when mixed with hard alcohol. He left her body in her apartment for someone else to find.

Later Daniel was on a telephone call to Joan's parents. "She went downhill fast," he said. "No one knew she was that far gone." She was a respectable person with a huge heart. He left a final memory of her as a drug addict. This is what he did. He didn't just rob people and murder them. He stole their dignity.

# Kenneth Howard

The clerk at the post office leaned over the counter. She said, "We opened a post office box for your new roommate." Her wavy sandy red hair fell over her shoulder as she stretched forward in my direction. Sunlight brightly spilled through the picture window and glistened off the light gray counter, light gray tiled floors, and white painted walls. The lobby was too bright. The light grays sun bleached to white.

The post office wasn't busy. Only two people stood in line waiting for the clerk, a woman buying stamps and a man mailing a large package. However, they both turned their heads with wide eyes and waited to hear my response.

"You mean my daughter?" I asked. I was leaving the post office, but I turned and stopped to understand what the clerk meant.

"No," the clerk answered. "It was a man."

"No men are living at my house," I answered.

"They should verify," said a friendly woman with a smile who was entering the post office. I passed by her on my way out.

I renewed my post office box for one full year. At the end of six months, I received a notice to renew my post office box. I took my receipt, and the amount charged to my checking account to the post office to show them the amount I paid. I checked the numbers; it was the annual fee.

The clerk at the post office cheerfully said, "We were told with apologies that you intended to renew your post office box for 6 months and renew on the other post office box for 6 months. We split the payment."

"What other post office box?" I asked. "I only have one PO box. Do you mean to tell me that you used part of my payment to renew someone else's PO box?" The clerk brought her supervisor to the front desk.

He was a tall man with brown eyes. He looked down at the amount, corrected the mistake, and placed a notice for renewal in the other PO box. "That's not a very nice guy, to have her pay on his box and not pay on hers," he mumbled. This was post office fraud, but the local police were not contacted.

I received an offer from Quicken Loans to refinance. The flyer advertised a lower interest rate. I started the paperwork, but I did not complete it. I was apprehensive about the transaction. Later I received a call from Quicken Loans to complete the paperwork. I told them, "I don't want to sign until I know the interest rate will be less than my current loan."

Quicken Loans said, "We need to know how much money you want in the refinance."

"I don't want any extra money," I answered. "In the advertisement, you wrote that I could reduce my interest rate. That is what I'm replying to."

"We can't do that," Quicken Loans said. "It would be illegal." Later Quicken Loans called back, "How much of your home value is owned by your ex-husband."

"I am the sole owner," I responded. "Only my name is on the deed and title."

"Yes, but," Quicken Loans continued, "what percentage of the house is owned by your ex-husband."

"He doesn't own any of the house," I answered. "Zero percent," I clarified.

"I mean for living there," Quicken Loans clarified.

"My ex-husband has never lived here," I responded. "We separated in 1999. He lives in Yakima."

"He might live in Yakima now," Quicken Loans said, "But how long did he live with you?"

"No one has lived with me at my house," I replied. "My ex-husband is a Yakima man. He was born in Yakima. He was raised in Yakima. He has never lived anywhere but in Yakima. And he intends to die in Yakima."

"We are trying to figure out how much of your home is owned by your ex-husband so that we know how much we can lend to him," Quicken Loans clarified.

"Don't lend anything to him," I instructed. "I am the sole owner of the home, my home."

"It might be a different ex-husband," Quicken Loans said. "Have you been married to someone else?"

"A very long time ago," I replied. "He doesn't live anywhere near here."

"What would you say if I told you he lives near, very near," Quicken Loans asked.

"I'd call the police," I responded.

"Then I won't tell you," Quicken Loans said. That ended the call.

Later I received a call from the FBI, "Whatever you do, don't sell your house." The FBI warned, "Your ex-husband already spent the money in anticipation that he'll be getting it."

"I don't understand," I answered.

"That's all the information I can give you." As odd as this call might be, I had grown accustomed to receiving them. I avoided any temptation or suggestion to sell. This is even though I received more calls from realtors to sell my home than all other calls combined.

I recorded this conversation:

History is on. Messages sent with history on are saved. Updating.
Thursday, Jun 10, 2021

Kenneth Howard
Jun 10, 2021, 7:25 PM
Let's chat on Hangouts!

Karen
Jun 12, 2021, 10:04 PM
I'm not sure how to use this, but I'll give it a try.

Kenneth Howard
Jun 12, 2021, 10:04 PM
Wow, I caught you babe. Welcome to hangouts! It's more fun here.

Karen
Jun 12, 2021, 10:06 PM
Okay. Maybe your connection is better with this platform.

Kenneth Howard
Jun 12, 2021, 10:07 PM
Oh yes. So, what do you intend doing right now?

Karen
Jun 12, 2021, 10:08 PM
The strawberry jam is done. I need to get my daughter's cat secured indoors. Otherwise, I'm just sitting in the living room.

Kenneth Howard
Jun 12, 2021, 10:09 PM
Wow

Karen
Jun 12, 2021, 10:10 PM
It is raining cats and dogs outside.

Kenneth Howard
Jun 12, 2021, 10:10 PM
Oh, I see. I prefer dog to cat. But I don't keep pets.

Karen
Jun 12, 2021, 10:10 PM
I'm a cat person. But I can get used to dogs.

Kenneth Howard
Jun 12, 2021, 10:11 PM
Smile

Karen
Jun 12, 2021, 10:11 PM
I live next to a wildlife refuge. So, I'm used to seeing and hearing animals everywhere. Seems strange without them.

Kenneth Howard
Jun 12, 2021, 10:11 PM
I like that. It's good to keep lively always. I don't like doll moment because its make not to think straight. I am tired of seeing dead bodies here right now.
*[Where was he seeing dead bodies, if he never seemed to go to work and never went out?]*

Karen
Jun 12, 2021, 10:13 PM
I know what you mean. I'll try to find some happy, up-lifting stories for you to fuel you back up.
Service professions always need a pick-up source to get back on track.

Kenneth Howard
Jun 12, 2021, 10:15 PM
I would be very glad.

Karen
Jun 12, 2021, 10:16 PM
What do you have planned today?

Kenneth Howard
Jun 12, 2021, 10:16 PM
I really need someone as special as you to cheer me up here
Gym by 9 AM

Karen
Jun 12, 2021, 10:17 PM
Okay, I'll keep that in mind. Do you like to go to the gym?

Kenneth Howard
Jun 12, 2021, 10:18 PM
Oh yes. I take lonely walks too.

Karen
Jun 12, 2021, 10:19 PM
I like lonely walks. I watch the birds and the squirrels.

Kenneth Howard
Jun 12, 2021, 10:21 PM
Pretty cool

Karen
Jun 12, 2021, 10:21 PM
A message about compassion

Kenneth Howard
Jun 12, 2021, 10:21 PM
Lovely pictures You are so romantic.

Karen
Jun 12, 2021, 10:25 PM
Trust in God.

Kenneth Howard
Jun 12, 2021, 10:26 PM
Yes, I am a strong Christian.

Karen
Jun 12, 2021, 10:27 PM
I read the Bible and like to study with others.

Kenneth Howard
Jun 12, 2021, 10:27 PM
I am practicing Catholic Christian because I was raised by a military Christian solder.
It's a very good ideal to always stick with the key sword.

Karen
Jun 12, 2021, 10:27 PM
Your father was in the army?

Kenneth Howard
Jun 12, 2021, 10:28 PM
Nope
My father was preacher man.

Karen
Jun 12, 2021, 10:28 PM
Oh, you are a PK, pastor's kid.

Kenneth Howard
Jun 12, 2021, 10:28 PM
Oh yes. He was a great Icon during his time. Well recognized known preacher

Karen
Jun 12, 2021, 10:29 PM
My father worked on cars. You must have been in the limelight often.

Karen
Jun 12, 2021, 10:34 PM
What was your father's name? Did he work in the UK or Ireland?

Kenneth Howard
Jun 12, 2021, 10:35 PM
Germany Taylor Do you still have your parents alive?

Karen
Jun 12, 2021, 10:37 PM
My parents are alive. They are in their 80s.

Kenneth Howard
Jun 12, 2021, 10:38 PM
Oh great.

Karen
Jun 12, 2021, 10:38 PM
When do you leave for the gym?

Kenneth Howard
Jun 12, 2021, 10:39 PM
When is your birthday?

Karen
Jun 12, 2021, 10:40 PM
I'm glad you have a gym to work out at. My birthday is in 1 month, July 12th.

Kenneth Howard
Jun 12, 2021, 10:42 PM
Mine is Aug 2

Karen
Jun 12, 2021, 10:42 PM
Do you have a birthday coming up? Oh, I see. I'll put that on my calendar.

Kenneth Howard
Jun 12, 2021, 10:42 PM
Lori's birthday is fast approaching.

Karen
Jun 12, 2021, 10:43 PM
She would enjoy a phone call from you.

Kenneth Howard
Jun 12, 2021, 10:43 PM
Oh yes, as usual. I still did not let her know about our meeting yet, what do you think?

Karen
Jun 12, 2021, 10:45 PM
She doesn't need to know until our relationship is more established.

Kenneth Howard
Jun 12, 2021, 10:46 PM
Really If you say so no problem with me I want to ensure the best life for her She's the only family I have right now Karen, are you there?

Karen
Jun 12, 2021, 10:51 PM
My oldest daughter came home. She is talking with me about Egyptian games. My youngest daughter is talking about pictures made of chocolate.

Kenneth Howard
Jun 12, 2021, 10:55 PM
Okay, I think I have to leave you for now.

Karen
Jun 12, 2021, 10:56 PM
Okay. Thank you for understanding. I hope to connect with you again soon.

Kenneth Howard
Jun 12, 2021, 10:56 PM
Ok babe Always a good time with you

Karen
Jun 12, 2021, 10:57 PM
It is nice to spend time with you. Looking forward to seeing those green eyes.

Kenneth Howard
Jun 12, 2021, 10:57 PM
Smiles Chat you OK, HUGS

Karen
Jun 12, 2021, 10:58 PM
Hugs 💞

Karen
Jun 12, 2021, 11:00 PM
Nice to see you "smile."

Kenneth Howard
Jun 13, 2021, 7:59 AM
Good morning to you. May every step you make be filled with happiness, love, and peace.

Kenneth Howard
Jun 13, 2021, 4:02 PM
I hope all is well, fine and ok with you?

Karen
Jun 13, 2021, 8:21 PM
Hi. All is fine here. The cherries are ready to pick, but small this year. I hope I didn't miss you before you need to leave for work. Thank you for the lovely blue roses. Blue roses mean mystery and attaining the impossible. Thank you for the early morning greetings too.

Karen
Jun 13, 2021, 8:31 PM
I set up Google alerts, but didn't get an alert. I apologize. I am learning. I hope you have a good day at work.

Kenneth Howard
Jun 13, 2021, 8:34 PM
Apologies accepted.

Karen
Jun 13, 2021, 8:34 PM
I see you are at the computer. When do you need to leave for work this morning?

Kenneth Howard
Jun 13, 2021, 8:34 PM
So how was your day like because I really did miss you
I will leave for work in few hours.

Karen
Jun 13, 2021, 8:35 PM
I'm fine. I went to church. My first in person experience in a very long time. It was so wonderful, I almost cried with joy. So nice to feel His spirit.

Kenneth Howard
Jun 13, 2021, 8:36 PM
Wow beautiful, I really did miss a lot.

Karen
Jun 13, 2021, 8:36 PM
I watched a movie with my daughters. My last chance before ----- leaves. I missed you too.

Kenneth Howard
Jun 13, 2021, 8:37 PM
Now I know the reason I didn't hear from you.

Karen
Jun 13, 2021, 8:37 PM
I checked Facebook and my email. No alerts or messages. I didn't check here.

Kenneth Howard
Jun 13, 2021, 8:38 PM
Alright but please always try and check your message every morning and evening your time okay.

Karen
Jun 13, 2021, 8:39 PM
Okay. Thank you for catching the 8 am time. That was 6 pm your time.

Kenneth Howard
Jun 13, 2021, 8:40 PM
I will always do anything for you. I hope you ate dinner?

Karen
Jun 13, 2021, 8:42 PM
We had prawns with Spanish rice

Kenneth Howard
Jun 13, 2021, 8:42 PM
It sounds delicious. What's the time over there?

Karen
Jun 13, 2021, 8:43 PM
The prawns were on spits with peaches and green onions. It is 8:43 pm here.

Kenneth Howard
Jun 13, 2021, 8:44 PM
That's good.

Karen
Jun 13, 2021, 8:45 PM
We had clear weather yesterday. Today mostly rain. We did pick some cherries before they split.

Kenneth Howard
Jun 13, 2021, 8:46 PM
That's good. I'm 55 years old and you?

Karen
Jun 13, 2021, 8:46 PM
I'm 55 years old too. Not yet menopausal though.

Kenneth Howard
Jun 13, 2021, 8:47 PM
Lovely So, tell me what's your favorite food, color, drink and movie?

Karen
Jun 13, 2021, 8:48 PM
My favorite color is indigo. My favorite food is halibut. My favorite drink is hard cider. My favorite movie would be something old . . . I'll need to think. And you?

Kenneth Howard
Jun 13, 2021, 8:49 PM
You are so sweet and funny. Lol

Karen
Jun 13, 2021, 8:49 PM
I really liked Prince of Persia

Kenneth Howard
Jun 13, 2021, 8:50 PM
I love turkey rice casserole, red for roses and white for peace, champagne, red wine and Star Wars.
*[These are clues. The first part of the conversation threw me off.]*

Karen
Jun 13, 2021, 8:50 PM
I think it is a good line when he says, "Bought her for the price of a camel. Look at her. She is worth at least two." Princess Leia, I'm thinking of the Carrie Fisher memorial.

Kenneth Howard
Jun 13, 2021, 8:52 PM
Beautiful Yes, that's also very nice

Karen
Jun 13, 2021, 8:53 PM
What type of champagne do you like?

Kenneth Howard
Jun 13, 2021, 8:54 PM
Moet and Chandon
[Another clue I missed.]

Karen
Jun 13, 2021, 8:54 PM
I usually have Angry Orchard hard apple cider.

Kenneth Howard
Jun 13, 2021, 8:54 PM
That's nice.

Karen
Jun 13, 2021, 8:55 PM
I think of white as purity, instead of peace. But I like the imagery of peace for white.

Kenneth Howard
Jun 13, 2021, 8:56 PM
Yes, it also signifies purity and pure heart okay. All my life I have been visiting different orphanage homes to support the orphans and less privileged and also pray with them, since my divorced I have been traveling to different countries to visit orphanage homes praying with the kids and giving them financial support. I have been so lonely since my divorce and I have been praying to God almighty to answer my prayer's in finding a woman in my life that I will love for all eternity as much as she will forever love me in return, so we can live happily together forever as one loving family.

Karen
Jun 13, 2021, 8:57 PM
God is faithful.

Karen
Jun 13, 2021, 9:01 PM
Do you have any pictures of yourself or where you are located?

Karen
Jun 13, 2021, 9:04 PM
Do you need to know whether I would forever love you?
I'm the type of person who fixes a 1940 sewing machine instead of buying a new one.

Kenneth Howard
Jun 13, 2021, 9:06 PM
No, I really don't have any recent pictures here because here in the war zone, we are not allowed to take photos, make calls, video chat or perform any kind of cell activities because the rebellions are using any kind of trackers to get to use, and I don't want to lose my job okay.
Yes, I really want to know if you would love me and my daughter forever okay.

Karen
Jun 13, 2021, 9:07 PM
Wow! You are so gorgeous. I understand about your job.
I had similar restrictions at Hewlett Packard and when the Navy considered hiring me.

Kenneth Howard
Jun 13, 2021, 9:08 PM
Thanks for the compliment.
I pray your interview goes well for your tomorrow.

Karen
Jun 13, 2021, 9:09 PM
Yes, I need to learn the 14 principals of Amazon and think up scenarios for each one.

Kenneth Howard
Jun 13, 2021, 9:09 PM
Can you please me a little more on your Amazon job?
*[I usually do my best to avoid answering questions about my job.]*

Karen
Jun 13, 2021, 9:12 PM
Right now, I just pick from yellow pods and transfer warehouse goods to yellow totes, then transfer warehouse goods from yellow totes to gray trays, and then transfer warehouse goods from gray trays to white chutes. I used to put warehouse goods into boxes for shipping. The -----

Kenneth Howard
Jun 13, 2021, 9:14 PM
Wow that's a very nice job. I hope you do have a good pay?

Karen
Jun 13, 2021, 9:14 PM
It is okay. Below my skill level. But there is no such thing as "overqualified" at Amazon.
I make good pay when I work overtime hours, which is nearly every week.

Kenneth Howard
Jun 13, 2021, 9:16 PM
So, you mean you are paid weekly?

Karen
Jun 13, 2021, 9:16 PM
Does the UN pay you well? Usually they do, don't they, and it is just the work conditions that aren't so good. I get paid weekly at Amazon.

Kenneth Howard
Jun 13, 2021, 9:19 PM
Yes, the UN does pay me very well. The contract I'm currently working on right now is worth over $500,000 and i do receive $5000 monthly that is been sent to my account in the states.
So, tell me how much do you receive weekly?

Karen
Jun 13, 2021, 9:21 PM
Is it dry in Yemen? Or raining? I'm thinking it is desert like. My pay varies with the overtime hours and whether we have a peak. I might only receive $500/week. Or more, depending on their need

Kenneth Howard
Jun 13, 2021, 9:22 PM
It's dry and always sunny here in Yemen.

Karen
Jun 13, 2021, 9:22 PM
That is what I thought. And many people without food, needing assistance.

Kenneth Howard
Jun 13, 2021, 9:23 PM
Yes, the UN are really doing a great job here in Yemen.

Karen
Jun 13, 2021, 9:23 PM
Is Saudi Arabia helping there?

Kenneth Howard
Jun 13, 2021, 9:23 PM
Yes, a little but the UN are doing a very great over here Do you have siblings?

Karen
Jun 13, 2021, 9:25 PM
I have two sisters. We are estranged. My childhood was rocky. I became close to the neighbor's family and later was in foster care.

Kenneth Howard
Jun 13, 2021, 9:26 PM
I'm so glad you also have your sisters around you. What about your parents?

Karen
Jun 13, 2021, 9:27 PM
My parents live close by. My father is close to my older sisters. The middle sister is his favorite. That all falls into a dark story I'd rather save for later

Kenneth Howard
Jun 13, 2021, 9:27 PM
Alright dear

Karen
Jun 13, 2021, 9:28 PM
It is 7:28 am Monday morning over there. Do you need to get dressed and ready for work?

Kenneth Howard
Jun 13, 2021, 9:29 PM
My dad is from Nuess Germany while my mom is an America from Alabama. So am an America citizen with an accent. Yes, I will leave for work at 8am okay.

Karen
Jun 13, 2021, 9:29 PM
Oh, I see. I'm sure it is a lovely accent.
We have a little time before you need to get dressed, hair brushed, teeth brushed, and heading out the door.

Kenneth Howard
Jun 13, 2021, 9:31 PM
Yes, you are gonna love it. I'm the only child of my parents. I lost my parents when I was 16 years old. Since then, I have been working for myself. Yes, we still got some minutes left.

Karen
Jun 13, 2021, 9:32 PM
That must have been interesting losing your parents before finishing high school.
Sometimes these things make us strong. God is always holding us and giving us a hug. Sometimes we just don't see it.

Kenneth Howard
Jun 13, 2021, 9:33 PM
Yes, and I'm so proud of myself today.

Karen
Jun 13, 2021, 9:33 PM
You've accomplished much.

Kenneth Howard
Jun 13, 2021, 9:34 PM
Yes, by the special grace of God.

Karen
Jun 13, 2021, 9:34 PM
I'm happy you held onto your roots and built something higher.

Kenneth Howard
Jun 13, 2021, 9:35 PM
Thank you very much. So, tell me what do you like about a man?

Karen
Jun 13, 2021, 9:36 PM
I like a sense of humor, mainly easy going, protective, a good listener, compassionate, sexually passionate. Honest, hard-working, educated, loving God, and willing to put up with me.

Kenneth Howard
Jun 13, 2021, 9:37 PM
You sound so sweet and adore you a lot.

Karen
Jun 13, 2021, 9:38 PM
Thank you. I'd give you a big hug if I could.

Karen
Jun 13, 2021, 9:40 PM
You are a wonderful man.

Kenneth Howard
Jun 13, 2021, 9:41 PM
Thanks for the compliment. Do you still want a man in your life?

Karen
Jun 13, 2021, 9:43 PM
Yes, I need a man in my life. It has been a long, lonely time, but that just makes me more appreciative.

Kenneth Howard
Jun 13, 2021, 9:45 PM
You sound so great, I really do want a woman in my life to love me and my daughter forever, as much as I will forever love her and together is where we should be for all eternity.

Karen
Jun 13, 2021, 9:46 PM
I'd like to see if we can make it work. I think we need to get to know each other more.

Kenneth Howard
Jun 13, 2021, 9:46 PM
Yes, that's why asking you these questions okay

Karen
Jun 13, 2021, 9:47 PM
Okay

Kenneth Howard
Jun 13, 2021, 9:47 PM
So, tell me what kind of a man would you love to spend the rest of your life with?

Karen
Jun 13, 2021, 9:48 PM
I suppose he would need to put up with me.

Kenneth Howard
Jun 13, 2021, 9:50 PM
You sound so sweet; I want to spend the rest of my life with a God-fearing Lady that will forever love me and my daughter and that she will treat her like her own child.

Karen
Jun 13, 2021, 9:50 PM
I would be happy to treat a 12-year-old girl as my own child.

Kenneth Howard
Jun 13, 2021, 9:51 PM
That's so sweet of you.

Karen
Jun 13, 2021, 9:52 PM
Does she have green eyes like you?

Karen
Jun 13, 2021, 9:53 PM
How adorable. So happy for dad. You only have a few minutes. You have a great day at work, okay?

Kenneth Howard
Jun 13, 2021, 9:54 PM
Yes, she's all I got, she means everything to me. My world. Are you willing to relocate for work?

Karen
Jun 13, 2021, 9:55 PM
I could look into it. There are Amazon facilities all over the world.

Kenneth Howard
Jun 13, 2021, 9:56 PM
That's a good idea.

Karen
Jun 13, 2021, 9:57 PM
Be safe at work and keep focused on happy thoughts.

Kenneth Howard
Jun 13, 2021, 9:57 PM
I also want you to know I'm willing to relocate to any where I find true love, buy a new house and start a new living of a complete man with my soulmate living together as one lovely family.

Karen
Jun 13, 2021, 9:58 PM
Thank you. I am living in the sticks here. But it is lovely with rivers nearby.

Kenneth Howard
Jun 13, 2021, 9:58 PM
That's good. Do you still believe in true love?

Karen
Jun 13, 2021, 10:00 PM
I still believe in true love.

Kenneth Howard
Jun 13, 2021, 10:01 PM
You sound so sweet. I so much believe in love and I know that someday I will find true love that will last for a life time.

Karen
Jun 13, 2021, 10:05 PM
Have a good day. I'll chat with you again after you get off work.

Kenneth Howard
Jun 13, 2021, 10:20 PM
Alright dear. I will text you on my break okay. Please always do check your Hangout okay. Have a good night sleep, sweet dreams.

Kenneth Howard
Jun 14, 2021, 5:23 AM
It is very important to start your day with a positive affirmation. You are the greatest gift of the universe. You are loved and appreciated. You are unique and beautiful. I know this day will bring you a lot of happiness. Good morning sweetie.

Karen
Jun 14, 2021, 8:18 AM
Good Morning. I was up early getting ready for my job interview today and went back to sleep. You might be getting off work soon. We'll get this down.
Positive affirmation: You are a child of God. God works for to the good for those who love Him and are called to His purpose.
I'm certain you are in God's purposes there in Yemen. He loves you and loves the work you are doing with His people who are in the most need.

Kenneth Howard
Jun 14, 2021, 8:22 AM
I pray you pass the interview and get the job, just believe in God okay.

Karen
Jun 14, 2021, 8:23 AM
Yes, I'll trust. I would think, "It will be okay if I don't get it. I'll try again later." But I need to realize this is my primary opportunity and if I don't do well, I might not get another.

Karen
Jun 14, 2021, 8:25 AM
Are you off work or on duty?

Kenneth Howard
Jun 14, 2021, 8:25 AM
Yes, that's it. Opportunity comes but once okay. I'm currently working but I missed you so much, so I had to come check on you.

Karen
Jun 14, 2021, 8:26 AM
Thank you. I'm preparing scenario answers to their 14 principals.

Kenneth Howard
Jun 14, 2021, 8:28 AM
Wow that's great. I hope am not interrupting anything.

Karen
Jun 14, 2021, 8:33 AM
You aren't interrupting much. I'm just getting myself breakfast.
I thought I would warm up the gluten-free pancakes I made yesterday, but my daughter ate them before she went to work this morning. So, I'm making something else.
*[My daughter denied eating the pancakes. "Why would I eat gluten-free pancakes," she retorted. I believe her. Someone else was in my house and in my refrigerator, eating my food.]*

Kenneth Howard
Jun 14, 2021, 8:35 AM
Alright, you must be very good at baking.

Karen
Jun 14, 2021, 8:41 AM
I enjoy baking. I've been a baker for 49 years.

Kenneth Howard
Jun 14, 2021, 9:07 AM
Lovely
I would really love to taste your pancakes.

Karen
Jun 14, 2021, 9:14 AM
I was planning to put the new strawberry jam. But decided on maple syrup. I'm back to studying. And ready to take a break.

Kenneth Howard
Jun 14, 2021, 11:42 AM
That's good.
So, what are you doing right now?

Karen
Jun 14, 2021, 4:44 PM
I took a nap, because I'll be awake until 6am. I fixed myself dinner and I'll be heading out soon.
If I don't hear from you between now and when I go to the interview, I'll let you know in the morning how it went. (About 6am my time is 4pm your time.)

Kenneth Howard
Jun 14, 2021, 4:54 PM
I pray you get the job okay. Much love

Karen
Jun 14, 2021, 4:57 PM
Thanks!

Kenneth Howard
Jun 14, 2021, 4:57 PM
Big hugs

Karen
Jun 14, 2021, 4:58 PM
Big hugs back to you!

Kenneth Howard
Jun 15, 2021, 4:06 AM
Good morning to my best friend! It's time to wake up and do something important for this world. I know you are capable of anything. Let's make this planet a better place for everyone. Rise and shine!

Karen
Jun 15, 2021, 6:00 AM
Hi! My job interview went well. I was given a few questions and asked to respond with the S.T.A.R. method. I've forgotten what that stands for. But I think it has something to do with telling a story of an accomplishment for each question. So that is what I did.

Kenneth Howard
Jun 15, 2021, 6:01 AM
That's good, I believe you, you will come out best okay.

Karen
Jun 15, 2021, 6:01 AM
I hope if I don't get it this round, they will keep me in mind for the next round.

Kenneth Howard
Jun 15, 2021, 6:02 AM
You will get it, just believe in what God can do okay.

Karen
Jun 15, 2021, 6:02 AM
Yes, God has got this. ----- leaves today.

Kenneth Howard
Jun 15, 2021, 6:04 AM
That's good. Have you taken coffee?

Karen
Jun 15, 2021, 6:04 AM
She came as a surprise visit and stayed for over a month. I haven't had coffee yet. I'll need to get some rest soon. I was up all-night working. We are getting ready for Amazon prime day. So, we are getting moved to different stations.

Kenneth Howard
Jun 15, 2021, 6:07 AM
Wow that's good.

Kenneth Howard
Jun 15, 2021, 6:07 AM
Beautiful sunset

Karen
Jun 15, 2021, 6:08 AM
Yes, beautiful. A friend of mine from 8th grade takes photos of the area. This is one of his.

Kenneth Howard
Jun 15, 2021, 6:08 AM
Wow it's so beautiful!

Karen
Jun 15, 2021, 6:08 AM
He took the photos of the eagles too.
I try to stay in contact with friends from school. They are like extended family to me.

Kenneth Howard
Jun 15, 2021, 6:09 AM
Yes, that's a very good idea
Will you ever committed in a relationship and want it to last for a lifetime?

Karen
Jun 15, 2021, 6:11 AM
Yes, of course I want it to last a lifetime. I want my heart to be broken if it ends. I want to love that deeply.

Kenneth Howard
Jun 15, 2021, 6:14 AM
You sound so sweet, and I really wait to spend the rest of my life with you

Karen
Jun 15, 2021, 6:14 AM
We should continue to get to know each other. What is your favorite music?

Kenneth Howard
Jun 15, 2021, 6:15 AM
Kenny Roger, I will always love you.

Karen
Jun 15, 2021, 6:17 AM
I like Kenny Rogers too. You don't bring me flowers. You don't sing me love songs. You hardly talk to me anymore when I come through the door at the end of the day... Something to try NOT to do. Dolly Parton sang I will always love you. Oh, I guess it was another duet.
Dolly Parton & Kenny Rogers for I will always love you. Barbara Streisand & Kenny Rogers for You don't bring me flowers Wynona & Kenny Rogers for Mary did you know. I'm going to get some rest. Have a good rest of the day at work.

Kenneth Howard
Jun 15, 2021, 6:34 AM
Wow beautiful songs. Sleep tight and sweet dreams. Please do text me when you are awake, okay.

Kenneth Howard
Jun 15, 2021, 2:28 PM
Hello sweetie, I hope all is well, fine and ok with you?

Karen
Jun 15, 2021, 4:30 PM
Yes, I'm fine. ----- left for Colorado. It is sad. And so hard to reconnect when I do see her. I prepared dinner and will leave in a little over 30 minutes. How is your day going?

Karen
Jun 15, 2021, 4:43 PM
My favorite song is by Roni Dalumi from album Tistakel, called Osa Li Einaim

Kenneth Howard
Jun 15, 2021, 4:44 PM
Wow that's good. It's 2:45 AM over here and I just relaxing. I can't even sleep

Karen
Jun 15, 2021, 4:46 PM
Oh. I must have gotten my times messed up. What would help you go back to sleep?

Kenneth Howard
Jun 15, 2021, 4:48 PM
I just need you beside me sweetie.

Karen
Jun 15, 2021, 4:54 PM
Okay. I'm beside you. I'd sing you a lullaby if you could hear me. Sweet dreams.

Kenneth Howard
Jun 15, 2021, 6:34 PM
Thank you very much. Big hugs

Kenneth Howard
Jun 16, 2021, 3:53 AM
This day started with a beautiful morning, and I want to share this beauty with you, mate. I hope that this day brings you a lot of joy and happiness, because you are someone who deserves it. Rise and shine sweetie

Karen
Jun 16, 2021, 6:03 AM
Hi Kenneth. Thank you for the beautiful flowers and words of joy. I was thinking about you while I was working. I noticed thoughts of you made me a calmer person and more able to see the humor in things. You bring out the best in me.

Kenneth Howard
Jun 16, 2021, 6:04 AM
I'm so glad to hear it, you just made my day Have you eaten breakfast?

Karen
Jun 16, 2021, 6:04 AM
I'm eating breakfast now. Homemade granola with pecans and coconut and fresh blueberries.
You must have had lunch recently.

Kenneth Howard
Jun 16, 2021, 6:06 AM
That's sounds good and healthy.

Karen
Jun 16, 2021, 6:06 AM
It is a simple recipe.

Kenneth Howard
Jun 16, 2021, 6:07 AM
Yes, I ate pizza, veges and yoghurt What are you doing right now?

Karen
Jun 16, 2021, 6:07 AM
Wow! I'm eating breakfast. Then I'll do some stretches, shower, and go to bed.

Kenneth Howard
Jun 16, 2021, 6:11 AM
That's good. Do you have time so we can talk?

Karen
Jun 16, 2021, 6:12 AM
I have a little time. What's up?

Kenneth Howard
Jun 16, 2021, 6:15 AM
Do you really believe that you can possibly find that special man you would love to spend the rest of your life with someday?

Karen
Jun 16, 2021, 6:17 AM
Oh, course I believe that. I need to have hope. Relationships are work, but so rewarding/

Kenneth Howard
Jun 16, 2021, 6:19 AM
Yes, are absolutely right. Tell me dear, will you welcome the children of your dream man and treat them like your own children?

Karen
Jun 16, 2021, 6:19 AM
I will. My ex-husband had a 7-year-old daughter. I continue to treat her as my own daughter. She is now in her 30s.

Kenneth Howard
Jun 16, 2021, 6:24 AM
That's so sweet of you.

Karen
Jun 16, 2021, 6:24 AM
I'm going to slip in the shower now.

Kenneth Howard
Jun 16, 2021, 6:26 AM
Alright text me when you are done okay.

Karen
Jun 16, 2021, 6:31 AM
I'm back. All clean and legs shaved.

Kenneth Howard
Jun 16, 2021, 6:33 AM
That's good.

Karen
Jun 16, 2021, 6:33 AM
There was an Amazon customer who ordered at least 20 razors. I imagine she was covered with hair.

Kenneth Howard
Jun 16, 2021, 6:33 AM
Big hugs

Karen
Jun 16, 2021, 6:33 AM
Big hugs to you too

Kenneth Howard
Jun 16, 2021, 6:33 AM
You are so sweet and fun to be with I really can't wait to be home with you

Karen
Jun 16, 2021, 6:33 AM
Thank you. You are very sweet too. How much longer is your contract?

Kenneth Howard
Jun 16, 2021, 6:34 AM
In few months' time my contract will be over, I think maybe 4 months' time. I would really love to celebrate Christmas with you sweetie.

Karen
Jun 16, 2021, 6:35 AM
That would be nice. We have a small Christmas day here. I always have a tree and a nativity up.
I should get some rest soon.

Kenneth Howard
Jun 16, 2021, 6:37 AM
Alright sweetie

Karen
Jun 16, 2021, 6:37 AM
I'll text you when I wake up.

Kenneth Howard
Jun 16, 2021, 6:46 AM
Alright, sweet dreams about us. Big hugs

Karen
Jun 16, 2021, 4:20 PM
Flowers from my backyard to greet you when you awake. I hope you slept well.

Kenneth Howard
Jun 16, 2021, 5:59 PM
Yes, I slept very well thanks for asking How are you doing?

Karen
Jun 17, 2021, 6:07 AM
I'm doing fine. I'm trying to keep my eye on the "compassion beyond all understanding" part of God to show that towards others. (Instead of punching them in the face as I'm somewhat tempted to do.) I'm referring to work and those who hog the center lane. How does God feel towards them? Can I model that? I'm happy you slept very well! I hope your day is going well too.

[I didn't tell him this, but I recently got my car back from the repair shop. The car received 2 coats of paint. And I just noticed new scratches on the paint job. The scratches look intentional. A friend at work said, "Mark my words. The scratches happened because you were looking over the paint job."
"But then, the scratches would have happened while the car was parked in my driveway," I replied. I pause to think and dismiss his comment, "I live in a quiet neighborhood."]

Kenneth Howard
Jun 17, 2021, 6:13 AM
Yes, my day is going well but I really do miss you. Sweetie all I can tell you is that no one knows the mind of God okay.

Karen
Jun 17, 2021, 6:15 AM
I'm glad you are doing well today. Okay. I have one more day of work, then some time off.

Kenneth Howard
Jun 17, 2021, 6:15 AM
That's good news, so what will you be doing on your day of work?

Karen
Jun 17, 2021, 6:16 AM
On my day off, I'll look into what park I might go to. Are you off work this weekend?

Kenneth Howard
Jun 17, 2021, 6:18 AM
Yes, I'm off this weekend. So, tell me what do you like about a man?

Karen
Jun 17, 2021, 6:19 AM
I'll have more time to visit with you then. Do you have people there you get together with?
I'm going to drop off to bed soon. I'm a little tired.

Kenneth Howard
Jun 17, 2021, 6:21 AM
No, it's so lonely and bored here. The colleagues I have are always busy with their work.

Karen
Jun 17, 2021, 6:21 AM
Movies? Museums? Live music? Dancing? Do you like to dance?

Kenneth Howard
Jun 17, 2021, 6:22 AM
Here in the war zone, we don't go out. I'm always busy working and working.

Karen
Jun 17, 2021, 6:23 AM
I see. No walks in the moonlight.

Kenneth Howard
Jun 17, 2021, 6:23 AM
Yes, I like to dance only when I'm home, okay.
[Another clue]

Karen
Jun 17, 2021, 6:23 AM
Okay. I grew up in the 80s. So, I liked that music for dancing. Moving together in rhythm.

Kenneth Howard
Jun 17, 2021, 6:26 AM
That's very nice. So, tell me, what inspires you?

Karen
Jun 17, 2021, 6:26 AM
Did they have country music in Alabama or soft rock?

Kenneth Howard
Jun 17, 2021, 6:27 AM
Yes, they have country music.

Karen
Jun 17, 2021, 6:28 AM
What inspires me? Well people who study, pastors, teachers, rabbis, scientists, biologists, intellectual conversation. That was a poor sentence.

Kenneth Howard
Jun 17, 2021, 6:29 AM
Wow that's really amazing and inspiring.

Karen
Jun 17, 2021, 6:29 AM
I enjoy talking with experts in their field. Even if it is just about plants.

Kenneth Howard
Jun 17, 2021, 6:30 AM
That's good.
I'm inspired by God.

Karen
Jun 17, 2021, 6:31 AM
I'm inspired by God too. And Jesus. I should go off to bed soon. Super tired today.
I'll text you again later.

Kenneth Howard
Jun 17, 2021, 6:33 AM
Alright dear, sleep tight, sweet dreams.

Kenneth Howard
Jun 18, 2021, 5:49 AM
I wouldn't want a day to pass without me telling you how amazing you are and I wouldn't want this morning to pass without me wishing you a very sweet good morning. Have the best day yet!

Kenneth Howard
Jun 18, 2021, 5:55 AM
All my nights and days are filled with the wonders of your love. A lovely morning to you and thanks for being that special and wonderful woman in my life.

Karen
Jun 18, 2021, 6:47 AM
Thank you, Kenneth. That is very sweet. My oldest daughter just left for White Pass. So, I'll be on my own all week. I just finished my work week, but I haven't slept yet.

Kenneth Howard
Jun 18, 2021, 6:48 AM
Alright please get some rest but you seem to very tired

Karen
Jun 18, 2021, 6:52 AM
Yes, it has been a busy week. And next week will be busy too. But I'll have some time to chat.

Kenneth Howard
Jun 18, 2021, 6:52 AM
That's good. Have you taken coffee?

Karen
Jun 18, 2021, 6:59 AM
I had eggs with my daughter before she left. And I had some more granola with fresh blueberries. No coffee, but orange juice. It must be 5 pm there.

Kenneth Howard
Jun 18, 2021, 6:59 AM
Wow it sounds yummy! You are making me feel hungry.

Karen
Jun 18, 2021, 7:01 AM
Sorry. I should plan out my meals for the week before I go to the grocery store. What is your favorite dinner?

Kenneth Howard
Jun 18, 2021, 7:03 AM
That's good, when are you going to the grocery store? I love turkey rice casserole.
[Clue repeated]

Karen
Jun 18, 2021, 7:05 AM
I could buy some turkey. I'm going to rest, then I'll get laundry ready and stop by the grocery store on the way home. My washing machine transmission isn't working right, so I need to go to the laundromat.

Kenneth Howard
Jun 18, 2021, 7:06 AM
Alright sweetie but can you please do me a favor.

Karen
Jun 18, 2021, 7:07 AM
Sure thing

Kenneth Howard
Jun 18, 2021, 7:07 AM
Sweetie, can you please get me a steam card of 200 euros.

Karen
Jun 18, 2021, 7:08 AM
What is a steam card?

Kenneth Howard
Jun 18, 2021, 7:08 AM
I haven't heard from daughter Lori for some days now. It's a game gift card sweetie and Lori really needs it urgently.

Karen
Jun 18, 2021, 7:10 AM
She had her birthday earlier this month, didn't she?

Kenneth Howard
Jun 18, 2021, 7:11 AM
Yes, sweetie and she has been so upset me with me about the steam card.

Karen
Jun 18, 2021, 7:14 AM
You know that computer games are bad for their eyesight.

Kenneth Howard
Jun 18, 2021, 7:15 AM
Yes, she told me she doesn't want to use it for just the games, they have upcoming exams and it has a use

Karen
Jun 18, 2021, 7:17 AM
I don't know much about schools in Ireland and their use of steam cards. This seems out of my territory.

Kenneth Howard
Jun 18, 2021, 7:19 AM
Alright sweetie but can you please get it for me? I would really be glad and forever grateful to you if you can get it for me. I really do miss Lori so much.
Why the silence on me sweetie Are you upset with me, or you fell asleep? Hello sweetie.
Kenneth said he makes ten times more than I do. I'm trying to make ends meet. I need to pay to fix the transmission on my washing machine. And he wants me to buy him a 200 steam card!

  The next-door neighbor came over and knocked on my front door. "There was a man in your driveway on a computer," she said in a worried tone. "And I don't know if he was meant to be there."

  I looked out at the driveway with a sinking feeling. "Where?" I asked.

  "He was standing right on the other side of the fence," the neighbor said. "Balancing his laptop on your gate."

  A short man with blonde hair came by and asked me, "There is supposed to be a man here, right?"

  "No," I answered and shook my head.

  "That's not the reaction I expected you to have," he said as he ran towards Main.

A Saturday morning shortly after this, a car alarm was going off. The car was honking, beeping, and lurching. I thought, "Can't the neighbors do something about that blasted alarm? It was probably triggered by the wind. Why do we even have car alarms?" The sound came from across the street towards the west side.

My daughter entered the front door and asked me, "The neighbors are wondering why you don't do something about your car alarm."

"The car alarm?" I asked. "It's not my car alarm. It is across the street."

"That's just what they said," my daughter replied, shrugging her shoulders. "Then they saw you get out of your car."

I gave my daughter a confused look, "I haven't been outside all morning."

My daughter said, "The car is in the driveway now." She looked at the key holder by the front door. "Where is the key?" She asked me.

"What key?" I answered.

"The spare key to your car," my daughter answered. "Why did you get that thing anyway?"

"In case I lock my keys in the car," I answered. I looked at the key holder and couldn't find it. "Maybe it is in the drawer below." I started to dig through the drawer expecting to see the key at the bottom. I was lost in thought going through the old items.

"And why are the curtains closed?" my daughter asked. I looked up at the curtains in confusion. She looked at me going through the items in the drawer. "I can't believe it. You forgot what you were looking for."

Later the car key was back on the holder but stuck on the end of the fourth hook. Its location made the long key hang at an angle. I moved the key and the keychains to station the key on the back of the holder. This helped the items lay flat while hanging on the hook.

"The key will just move to the front again," my daughter told me.

I turned my head sharply to look at my daughter. My eyebrows were pressed low on my forehead. "How?" I asked.

"I don't know," my daughter answered. "It just does."

It was July 4, 2021, I worked a half day. I drove into work, taking the backroads. I expected the Fourth of July traffic to block access to my driveway when I returned home. However, I was relieved to find my driveway clear. Visitors were returning to their vehicles. One couple in a black SUV was angry about being charged a fee to park. A tall slender woman with shoulder-length sandy hair said to me, "Your landlord charged us $5 to park, even though this is the street."

"I don't have a landlord," I was offended and explained. "I'm a homeowner." "Lee said he was charging money all the way down." Lee accepted payment for cars to park along the north side of the road.

"I know Lee. It wasn't Lee," the woman said "It was an old man. He was balding. I'd show a picture of him to see if you recognize him if I had taken a picture."

Later a man scolded the couple, "It is one reason to know the people whose house you are parking in front of."

"I'm more offended he didn't give her the money," the woman said.

# Lawrence Otto Olsen

## Otto Spelled Backwards

Lawrence Olsen was born in September 1939. When Lawrence was a teenager, a new family moved into the neighborhood near their dairy farm. They had farmland, but no house to live in. Lawrence, his father, and his younger brother prepared to build a farmhouse for the new family. They cut down a large tree that had a trunk more than 6 feet in diameter. A man from the lumber yard came to cut the tree into 2"x4"x44" boards. Without blueprints, they set out to build the house. They had to think outside the box. The entire house was built out of that single tree. Decades later the family kept the 6 feet wide tree stump in place in the yard as a reminder of the generosity, the generosity of the neighbors who built their house and the generosity of the tree that provided the lumber.

When Lawrence went to university, he majored in mechanical engineering. He was also on the wrestling team. One year he pre-qualified for the Olympics in wrestling. His wrestling career took so much time away from his classes that when he came back to campus, he had a test the next day on electromagnetic fields and waves. He never received a lecture on the subject. So, he went to the library and found a book on the topic. Unfortunately, the book was in German. He didn't know any German. He did his best to understand the book. He studied the pictures and diagrams. He took the test and gave all the right answers.

The professor failed him. "You didn't show your work," he said.

Lawrence responded, "Yes, my work is right here." He pointed to circles and arcs on his test paper.

"Show me," the professor said. He handed Lawrence a piece of chalk and leaned back to watch.

Lawrence then went up to the chalkboard and showed how he solved the electrical problems. He drew Smith circles instead of using math equations. The professor smiled. His classmates clapped. And the professor gave him an A. Lawrence was thinking outside the box.

When Lawrence opened an engineering business of his own, one of his first clients was a man in Alaska. The client's wife had died, and he didn't want to leave the two-story house. It had too many memories of her. At the same time, he could no longer walk up the stairs to his bedroom. Lawrence looked all around the building. It was completely landlocked. It was common to build a house next to a rock face in Alaska for protection from the weather. Finally, Lawrence noticed the staircase. It was sturdy and might be used for an elevator. After all those years of thinking outside the box, he was forced to think in the box. Lawrence was the first to design and put an elevator in the stairwell.

Lawrence bought a four-bedroom house and a new work truck. The lawn was plush green grass, perfectly trimmed along the edge of the landscaped backyard. Lawrence built a new smoker in the backyard and invited the family and the neighbors for a barbeque.

My mother asked, "Did you see Lawrence's truck? It's in the driveway." There were several vehicles in the driveway. I landed my eyes on a newer-looking truck. "No, not that one. This one." Lawrence's truck was parked off to the side in the driveway next to a pile of bark dust. It was red. The truck didn't impress me. It was too large. "It's a work truck," she explained.

When my grandfather turned seventy years old, we had a birthday party. Lawrence arrived in his truck. "His smoker is so large, he was able to roast a full pig while he was driving on his way here," my mother beamed. "Do you want to see?" she asked. I passed. I regret not taking a second look at his truck.

Lawrence ran into legal problems at his business. Someone stole his elevator design drawings and sold them to an engineering firm. Now Lawrence was unable to build the design he created. The county filed a judgment. The problem took a while to sort out. Lawrence was left with a poor experience with the government.

## Skeleton is Found

A family left a note on the front door of my parents' house saying they were interested in buying the property. The property was not listed for sale. My father called them. They told my father they were interested in keeping the property as it is and not developing it. My father loved God's handiwork in the trees. He expected the old growth forest would remain. He agreed to sell.

The buyer approached my mother with the completed paperwork for the sale and said, "Your husband wants you to sign this." My mother was not consulted for the sale, even though it was her property. My mother was gifted property by her parents in exchange for care in their old age. She was to safeguard the acreage for the family. She included my father on the deed, which wasn't what her parents had wanted. My mother wanted to protect the property if she were to die. This was property she cherished. Nonetheless she signed the paperwork.

The new neighbors rented a large backhoe. They used their backhoe to remove the forest my father loved. They got rid of the timber. They cut down all the trees, pulled up the roots, and burnt the remains. They leveled the land to create "possibilities". But the tree roots weren't the only thing they dug up. The new neighbor's backhoe pulled up a dead body. In the act of pulling up the roots, they dug up a skeleton.

Our family discussed the situation. "Was it wearing clothes?" I asked. "Bodies decompose at a different rate than fabric." My mother looked at me like I was missing the point. It seemed like a practical question. The human body can decompose in about a year in ordinary soil. Fabric is different.

I imagine a moth eating away wool fabric. It must be like a gently broiled filet mignon with a glass of Chateau St. Michelle Chardonnay. And then the moth bites into a strand of polyester. It must taste like vomit in comparison. Poor moth. If the body is buried six feet under, there is no moth to eat the fabric at all.

Other bugs aid in decomposition. Cotton decomposes quickly, in one week to five months. Linen will decompose in only two weeks. Polyester takes 20 to 200 years to decompose. Rubber-soled boots decompose in 50 to 80 years.

A deer hunter may have been in the forest. They used the land for hunting. A deer hunter wears boots. Wasn't the person wearing shoes? Did someone bury a person without their shoes? Their clothing is a clue to who it is and when they were buried. Isn't anyone interested in more clues?

The skeleton is not Lawrence, it can't be. I invite Lawrence to my house every Thanksgiving and Christmas. He complained he had no one to leave an inheritance to. He was an intelligent man with a fascinating life. He had unusual accomplishments and a huge heart.

"Please write about Lawrence," my mother insisted. Her brother Lawrence was missing. She was worried. She was concerned that the skeleton the neighbors found was her brother Lawrence. Sometimes her instincts were right.

Maybe Lawrence was just trying to avoid his sister. It was entirely possible. They were never close. Growing up, if his sister wanted to play with dolls, Lawrence wanted to play with dolls too. Lawrence had his own doll. Once when his mother went into the store, the clerk offered to watch

Lawrence for her while she shopped for groceries. When his mother returned to the counter, Lawrence was holding a new boy doll. Lawrence's mother knew she would not be able to take the doll away from him. The clerk maneuvered the situation for Lawrence's mother to buy the doll. His mother complained, "There was a whole display of boy and girl dolls behind the counter. The clerk knew exactly what she was doing. The doll wasn't inexpensive either."

Lawrence's sister pretended to play with sticks and wood. In this way, she led Lawrence away from her. After encouraging him to play with something else, she went back to her dolls or whatever she wanted to do. Maybe this is the reason Lawrence became a contractor. He was led to design and construction. It was his new talent.

Just before Lawrence disappeared, an engineering company offered Lawrence two million dollars for his elevator design company. Lawrence tried to contact Steven, an old friend, to share some of the money. But Steven didn't return Lawrence's calls. This upset\ Lawrence. Lawrence couldn't figure out what he had done to offend Steven so badly.

Maybe Lawrence was enjoying the sale of his business. Once Lawrence took a trip to Bora Bora Bay, Tahiti with his parents. His mother complained, "Lawrence spent days staying in his room taking pictures of a woman on the beach in a bikini and doing nothing else. He planned to take the twelve best photos and make them into a calendar. The last day she came to the beach fully clothed. He decided he liked those pictures better." His mother decided not to bring him on trips with her again.

## The Lieutenant

The last time I saw Lawrence was on Thanksgiving Day 2014. I invited Lawrence to Thanksgiving dinner with me and my friend the lieutenant. Lawrence was familiar with a wide variety of subjects. He can have a good conversation with anyone. I anticipated that Lawrence and the lieutenant would enjoy each other's company.

The lieutenant was a tall man with pale skin and blue eyes. He was in the Navy for 19 years. He served in a couple of wars. The last war was in Afghanistan where he joined an army mission. His military truck was blown off the road by a hand grenade.

A neighbor drove Lawrence to my house. The driver used Lawrence's red truck. The neighbor pulled up just before my house and stopped across the street. The driver only showed his profile for the drop-off. He had pale skin. He didn't glance over at the house to ensure Lawrence was dropped off at the correct location. Most drivers pause to look at the house they stopped in front of. Or they look at the person they dropped off to make sure they are off the road before reentering traffic. Or they look down at their dashboard or down at their gear shift. Or make some sort of head movement. Or a polite greeting. Only his profile was visible as he drove off in Lawrence's truck.

The neighbor continued on to drive around the blind corner that leads to the main road. The corner isn't visible. Most people don't know the blind corner goes through to the main road. Most drivers assume it is a dead-end road and use driveways to turn around. The road didn't show on

Google Maps. The driver knew the area better than Google Maps and better than the city bus drivers.

[Later I learned the driver might have been Josh Searles who worked at Godfather's Pizza. Josh gave Lawrence rides. But that doesn't explain the mystery. Why didn't the driver turn his head? Is that a characteristic of pizza delivery drivers? Records show Josh was in Lawrence's neighborhood in 2022, not in 2014. Earlier information might be missing from the records.]

Lawrence is easy to be around. He isn't judgmental. Lawrence liked to help the underdog. Sometimes this meant taking on big government. At the dinner table, Lawrence told us how he helped a man in court in San Fransisco, California. He flew down in a friend's private jet. Two women lawyers came into the courtroom with a thick file. They were there to discredit Lawrence. Among other false accusations, they accused Lawrence of being a convicted wife beater.

I told Lawrence, "It doesn't make sense when you've never been married."

Lawrence said, "That part's not the point. They said convicted." He meant they didn't verify their information.

He explained the issue with the neighbors receiving confrontation as if they did not have a construction permit, "Her husband was away on business. She had a copy of the canceled check in her hands, three thousand dollars." Lawrence held out his hands as if holding a check. "These are my friends and reputable people." Lawrence explained, "There were two copies of the permit in the court file." Lawrence was bothered, "Why two copies?" He decided the judge would prefer if he spaced out the letters as if they were written by a typewriter.

I explained, "Judges prefer a Word document." Lawrence looked over at me, "I worked as a legal secretary one summer."

Lawrence shook his head and disregarded my advice. He said, "I found a woman who thinks she can do this with Excel. Each letter would be in its own cell, evenly spaced." The effect would mimic a typewriter. The document would look typed. This was an obsolete legal requirement, but it was still on the books. "Although she stopped coming around," Lawrence noted. "I'm not sure why." The report remained unfinished.

"There is probably a time constraint," I added nervously.

Lawrence frowned. He explained his own legal battle and why he was given a ride instead of driving himself. Lawrence was charged with a DIU, driving under the influence. His driver's license was suspended. It was a series of unfortunate events that caused him to lose his driver's license. We eagerly listened to Lawrence as he told the chain of events that led up to his plight. About six months before, he was invited to a party with old friends. The party was in a nearby town, in another county. He drank one beer and waited an hour before driving back home. He limited his alcohol intake to prevent problems with his heart. He was taking heart medication.

Lawrence was stopped by police who followed him. "An unusually large number of police pulled me over. They were out of their jurisdiction. So, they must have followed me." They stopped him for a DUI. They were from the jurisdiction with the permit issue. It was as if Lawrence was a victim of "swatting".

Lawrence had a court date coming up. His attorney kept delaying the court date. I explained to Lawrence this was a strategy lawyers used. The attorney plans to use the length of time you were without incident as a reason to dismiss or reduce the charges. It seems like negligence, but they are trying to help your case.

Lawrence requested a breathalyzer test or a blood test. He offered to pay the medical bill for a blood/alcohol test at the hospital. The police wouldn't allow the test. The evaluation of driving under the influence was subjective. "You can appreciate the math," Lawrence said to me. "How long does it take someone of my weight to process the alcohol in one beer?"

I explained, "We did this calculation in Unified Systems Bioengineering, simulating the organs of the body with math terms. The kidneys operate as a derivative process, while the intracellular fluid in the tissues operates as an integral process. Alcohol is processed in the kidneys, so the elimination is faster. Now there is usually a chart with the values already calculated."

"Exactly," Lawrence responded. The neighbor borrowed Lawrence's truck and gave him rides to where he needed to go.

"Your own personal Uber driver," the lieutenant replied with a smile. He summed it up nicely.

"I didn't tell him he could get into my tools," Lawrence added with aggravation.

"Is the neighbor someone you've known for a long time?" I asked. Lawrence lived in that neighborhood since I was very young. I remember going to visit Lawrence for the bar-b-que. He invited family and all the neighbors. To him the neighbors were family.

Lawrence shook his head. "Once and a while he stays when he doesn't have a place," Lawrence added with a shrug. He visualized being upstairs in his house, looking downstairs. After I pressed further, Lawrence admitted, "The neighbor stays in my house, downstairs." This wasn't a neighbor as much as it was a housemate. "It's a big house," Lawrence said defensively. He looked straight at me and used a definite tone as if he didn't want an argument.

I hadn't objected. I was only listening carefully. I tried to understand why Lawrence dodged my questions about his house guest.

"I don't think this is working," Lawrence said while looking down at his phone, expecting a text. "He's not getting back to me." He explained, "I told him he could use my truck. I never told him he could use my tools." He looked forward and his facial expression looked like he felt betrayed. He put his hand out for emphasis and said, "I have a toolbox in my truck."

"You mean the toolbox is in the backseat?" I asked.

Lawrence shook his head.

Lawrence looked down at his phone. He had a text message. "Wait, he's already here."

"That was quick," The lieutenant said with a surprised smile.

Lawrence paused in alarm, "I just thought of something. I didn't tell him where you live." He said softly, "He already knew."

The lieutenant was sitting next to the bay window and facing Lawrence. He immediately asked, "You mean for the pickup? Or the drop-off?"

"Either one," Lawrence replied. "I forgot to ask him if he had dinner plans," he added regretfully.

I explained to Lawrence, "You shouldn't need to walk one and a half blocks to meet him." I gestured towards the end of the block, "There is a bench at the corner."

Lawrence responded, "He said to pick me up on Main. I'd better go there." He immediately stood up out of the chair, went to the door, and began the walk down the road.

I mumbled, "I wanted to meet the neighbor."

The lieutenant replied, "So did I." The lieutenant was turned on the sofa with his right arm resting across the back. We both looked out the bay window as Lawrence walked up to the main road. We watched until Lawrence was out of sight. Then we glanced at each other.

"I would drive him home," the lieutenant said, "all he needed to do was ask."

I shrugged. "I would take him home too. And pick him up," I replied. "I would be glad to."

"I'm curious to find out what happens with the court case," the lieutenant said.

I nodded. I intended to follow it, but I had a flat tire to fix the day Lawrence went to court. I missed his hearing. I didn't think that would be my last opportunity to see him.

## Accepting the Mission

The situation was becoming suspicious. None of us heard from Lawrence, not even his younger brother. The police refused to take a missing person report. The police checked and the record said Lawrence's location was confidential. The police record gave me comfort that Lawrence was somewhere and okay. Maybe he didn't want to be disturbed.

The police said, "Lawrence's house appeared taken care of. It looked like a neighbor took care of the house while he was away. His mail was carefully stacked on the dining room table, expecting his return."

All of Lawrence's mail was on the table, except for my 2015 invitation for him to come to Thanksgiving dinner. That letter was marked "Return to Sender: Wrong Address." Why would my letter be marked as "Wrong Address"? Lawrence hadn't moved. Who marked the envelope? I'm wondering if Daniel was at Lawrence's house. Was he the mysterious housemate?

It was too late to check the handwriting. I tossed the envelope. Years ago, I tossed a letter I found on the floor in my bedroom closet. The paper was from a 6"x9" lined notepad, folded in half. The letter was addressed to my mother and said, "I don't know why Karen says those things about you. I really like you," and signed, "Dan." I couldn't make sense of why the letter was there. I assumed it was something to be thrown out decades ago. I tossed the letter into the trash, thankful that my parents were too smart to fall for Dan's manipulation.

## Wolf in Sheep's Clothing

Sometimes there is a wolf in sheep's clothing. Sometimes there is a sheep in wolf's clothing. Sometimes there is a sheep in sheep's clothing. Sometimes there is a wolf in wolf's clothing. The fine details of this necessary information were never explained to me. Instead, I was told that first impressions might be wrong.

Rita was 4'11" tall. She had black hair and dark brown eyes. She had polio as a child. She wore a brace on her foot and walked with a limp. I was encouraged to look at the beauty within. She had a soprano voice with vibrato.

Rita made sandwiches for blackberry pickers. She started making the sandwiches at 10:00 a.m. to feed the pickers at noon. Rita showed me the process. Two slices of white bread, spread with mayonnaise, and lunch meat. 'No lettuce or tomato?' I asked her.

"No that is all they get," Rita replied. I thought I would stay inside and help in the kitchen. "I don't need any help," she said. "You stay in the field and pick while I make the sandwiches."

I went out to the field to pick berries. The berries were small. It would take more to fill a flat. The bushes were yellow and brown. There was no shade. Later that morning, I looked and didn't find any outhouses in the berry field. I went to the house to use the bathroom.

Rita came out to the blackberry field. "Don't stop and use the bathroom!" Rita scolded. "You are wasting." Rita turned to her husband and said, "I can't believe this girl." She turned back towards me, "Look at the others. What do you think they do?" She turned her head and laughed, "If you need to pee just drop drawers and go in the aisle. You are young enough it won't make a difference."

In my head, I was thinking, "Why does she complain about me wasting time." It was my school vacation, and I was working. Picking blackberries at this farm was worse than when I was eight years old. At the other berry field, the big green leaves of the bushes provided shade from the hot sun and soaked up the heat from the rays. When the breeze came through, the wind rustled the leaves, and the scent of sweet berries wafted through the air. The berries were bigger and juicier. It didn't take long to fill a flat. When the flat was full, the weight of the flat was plenty, and the payout was good.

Here the bushes had small yellowing leaves. Some of the leaves were dry and brown. I was lucky if I had a chance to be on a row with green leaves. The berries were gray, withered, and dry. The berries were the type I was expected to pass over at the other berry farm. It took longer to fill a flat with these blackberries, and there was also more sun exposure while I worked. There were no bushes to soak up the heat from the sun.

I thought Rita would appreciate my hard work. Instead, I'm referred to as lazy. A large Hispanic man intently watched me as if he expected me to drop my pants. I got to work picking blackberries. I was thankful I already used the bathroom in the house.

After lunch, Rita apologized. The pickers who were mothers came up to her and told her they were appalled at the way she talked to me. I was shown another row to pick blackberries on. This row had green leaves on the bushes. There was a slight coolness. There was a spot of wet dirt on the end of the row, in front of the post that holds the berry supports.

"That row has just been watered," Rita said pointing down to the spot, "Step around it." She turned to her husband and said, "Sometimes she has no sense."

First, I'm referred to as lazy. Now I'm referred to as stupid. I viewed the landscape. There was no other spot watered except there. All other parts of the field were dry and dusty. It couldn't have been watered with a hose. I looked at both sides of the field. There was no hose, no piping, no faucet, no sprayer, no irrigation equipment. There was too much water for a bucket. Water from a bucket would spread differently and splash, with droplets turning over pockets of dry dusty earth as it poured out, before settling into the soil. There was no sign of a bucket. There was no bucket here and none where the full blackberry flats were turned in. Why was the soil wet here? The ground was so dusty, that walking through the wetter part of the soil would have been a cool relief. Instead, I was expected to go around the watered spot.

I looked up and back towards the neighbor's house. It was a pale green one-story ranch house with white trim. His house had a wooden fence around the yard. The grass in his yard was green, evenly mowed, and trimmed at the edges. There were no weeds. Green grass grew in the line between his car's tire tracks. In his driveway, the grass grew unless it was flattened. Even the neighbor's driveway had more water than the blackberry field. Why would the neighbor's driveway have more water than the blackberry field? The neighbor's driveway was uphill. Water flows downhill due to gravity. The only irrigation for the blackberry field was runoff from the neighbor watering his front lawn. The blackberry bushes grew best near there.

I asked Rita about the way the water spread on the dirt at the end of the blackberry row. She answered, "Oh, the ground is so hard, the water spreads out before it sinks into the soil."

"Why is there grass in the neighbor's driveway between his car's tire tracks?" I asked.

"The neighbor doesn't have a car, he drives a truck," Rita replied.

I changed my wording. "Don't you irrigate the garden?" I asked Rita.

"We irrigate the garden," Rita said with a smile. "That is how the blueberries are so large. They are the size of nickels." She proudly held the blueberries in her hands to show them off.

"Those are nice blueberries," I praised. "You should sell those," I suggested.

Rita made a disagreeable face and shook her head slightly. "Those are for eating," she said.

In my original question, I meant the blackberry field, not the garden. I changed the wording of my question. "Don't you irrigate the blackberry field?" I asked.

"The farm?" Rita asked for clarification. "Oh, he does his own irrigating," Rita said referring to her husband. She put canned goods away in the pantry as she talked. "It does save on water," she said, "for both one and two." She ducked back out of the pantry. Only her profile was visible. She gave an odd laugh.

At mealtime, Rita put a small scoop of rice in a metal ceremonial dish. She handed the rice to me and asked me to place the rice in the office in memory of Pops, her father-in-law. This was a Buddhist custom. The office was a small room under the staircase. The room had a strange smell. Pictures of young Asian women hung on the wall.

After the meal, Rita encouraged me to crack open a peach pit and eat the center. The peach pit had a bitter flavor. "It tastes like earwax," I complained.

"What would you know about the taste of earwax?" Rita laughed.

Rita's husband stood in the kitchen and complained, "A boy would have been better." He looked down and shook his head.

Rita quietly responded in a soprano voice, "She doesn't have any boys."

When my parents came to pick me up, I found out my sisters received a real vacation. When we got home to my mother I complained, "They were cross at me for going to the house to use the bathroom during picking time."

"They don't have outhouses," my mother observed. "There is only one bathroom in the house." My mother's eyes narrowed. "Is there a lineup at the house at breaks to use the bathroom?" she asked.

"No. They don't go to the house at all," I replied. "Rita brings them their lunch out in the field."

"They don't go to the house?" she asked. She grew up on a dairy farm. The farmhands all came to the house for breakfast, lunch, and dinner. Her mother stepped outside and rang her brass handbell to indicate when the meals were ready. All meals represented the four food groups. We were tested and graded on the food groups regularly. We knew them like the back of our hand, or better. The farm hands went indoors out of the hot sun. They gathered around the table, prayed and gave thanks to God for the meal, and dined together with dinner conversation. When they were thirsty, they drank fresh well water from the irrigation hose.

"No, they go straight to the berry field," I answered. "That is where they stay."

"They don't escape from the heat in midday," my mother asked. "Do they sit in the shade?"

"There is no shade, no trees," I answered. "They stay near their truck." I thought about it, "Their truck must provide some shade." They opened the truck doors to block some of the sun.

They eat without washing their hands?" my mother asked. She expected they would line up at the kitchen sink or go to the washroom to wash up before the meal the way they did at her parent's house.

"Yes, they must eat without washing their hands," I answered. "Maybe they wash their hands with drinking water, but I don't think so. They only receive one cup of water at lunchtime. They line up to get it. They bring their own cooler of water to drink."

"Why do they bring their own cooler of water?" she asked. She wondered why they didn't drink from the faucet or the hose.

"Rita said they've learned to," I answered and shrugged. That was all I knew.

My mother was thinking. "Do they pick berries without washing their hands?" Instinctively she knew the answer. Instead, she asked, "Are the berries washed?"

"No. Most of the berries go to the cannery for jam," I responded.

"That's why I make my own jam," my mother said. She went back to putting things away in the kitchen.

Later my mother said, "The cannery stopped taking the berries. They didn't have enough sugar content. Rita wondered how you get sugar into the berries."

"The farm was staffed with children and illegals," I replied.

"I don't remember you bringing home any money."

"I didn't." I explained, "Rita said I didn't make enough money to cover my room and board."

"As a perspective," my mother replied.

My father interjected, "All Rita knew about parenting was from watching our parents."

"They came out and looked at the farm," Rita complained. "They said we needed to put in bathrooms for the workers." She shook her head. "We'd have to put in a whole different system."

"Rita complained that she would be such a good mother," my mother said. "I thought if I gave you away to her, she would be so appreciative."

"All they had me do was work. And they complained that I was lazy," I explained. Rita complained I was wasting. I assumed she meant wasting time. "They staffed their berry farm with children and illegals."

"Did you spend time with the other children?" my mother asked.

"No," I answered. "They spent time with their families."

"We didn't think much about hiring illegals back then," my mother said. "You knew they needed the work." Later my mother commented about Rita, "Their farm was about to go bankrupt. They got an infusion of money from someplace."

# The Red Bag

In the bottom of the red overnight bag was my grandmother's brass handbell. She stepped out onto the front porch and rang the bell. This called the dairy farmhands to the house when meals were ready. Meals warm from the stove. Meals with the four food groups. Meals that started with a prayer and conversation, while men passed a pitcher of milk. Lawrence was a member of that dinner table.

Bread baked daily was topped with fresh turned butter and home canned preserves. Green tossed salad was made from vegetables in the garden. For dessert, berries were splashed with cream. The brass handbell represented those wholesome things. The brass handbell wasn't given to me, it was given to my mother. It is proof Daniel was in my parents' house! What else did he do? Who else did he visit? Where did he stay when he was in the area?

Another item in the red bag was a key. This looked like the key to my locker, which was broken into. The locker stored my rare coins, including one worth $167,000. The coin was given to me by my grandfather, Lawrence's father. It was stolen by Daniel.

Along with the other items was a door lock defeated with a jammed key. This bag held bragging rights. I discussed the contents of the red bag with the lieutenant.

"What year did Lawrence disappear?" the lieutenant asked.

"2015," I answered. It was the same year Jerry Taylor disappeared. The men were the same age.

"I had a feeling." The lieutenant's intuition kept him alive in war. "I am starting to believe the disappearance of the two men is connected." Each had a strange visitor just before the disappearance.

# Tests and Enemies

I was accustomed to strange visitors. A woman approached me at church. I'll call her Zephany. She stayed at a distance in the church entrance. This distance has the effect of involving as many bystanders as possible and destroying relationships. Even to people who know me well, Zephany claims she knows me better. I don't even know her real name, who she works for, or where she is getting her information.

"I'm getting my information from someone who is like a mother to you," Zephany said.

"I don't know who this person is that you refer to as my mother," I responded.

"I didn't say your mother," Zephany clarified. "Someone who is like a mother to you." She said with emphasis, "That's supposed to be a very good clue."

"It's not," I replied. I had no idea who she was talking about.

"A sister," Zephany said.

"My sisters aren't like mothers to me," I answered.

"I didn't say your sister," Zephany responded. I frowned.

"Doesn't it seem like I am talking with someone who knows you better than you know yourself?" Zephany pressed with a knowing smile.

"No, it seems like you are talking with a crackpot." I asserted.

"How can you talk that way about your mother?" Zephany asked in disgust.

At work, another woman stopped me on my way to the bathroom. I'll call her Zeddy. Zeddy approached me. "They told us what happened," she said. Daniel encouraged people to ask this question.

"Who are you referring to?" I asked. There was no subject in her sentence. The grammatical error was intentional.

"The man we were just talking about," Zeddy replied with a smirk.

Responses such as this give me a headache. I wrinkle my brow to ward off the on-coming pain. "If the sentence was written, it would be poor English. There are no context clues for the subject of the sentence." I explain this in clear English. I know she understands English.

"Can't you follow a conversation?" Zeddy chastised with a smirk. This conversation was a game to her.

"The private investigator, the man who ordered the private investigator report, the one who requested the private investigator report" I offered suggestions for the missing subject. I felt this was generous.

"The man you hurt," Zeddy replied.

"You are fishing," I said. There wasn't a man who I hurt.

"This is a fishing expedition," exclaimed a co-worker in the crowd. "You're accusing her of being ..." His voice fades as he is talking. I can't make out the last part of the sentence. It doesn't matter.

"It's been established," Zeddy snarled at him.

"No, it hasn't been established," I retorted. "It was disproven in the private investigator's report." I assume the man was saying "mentally ill" or a variety of other allegations. The private investigator's report showed I wasn't guilty of committing a crime and social services never had cause to start this harassment in the first place.

"You killed Jerry Taylor," Zeddy accused.

"I wouldn't have the ability to. I can't swim. I mean, I can't swim at all," I spoke the words "at all" slowly, my hands palms down, moving horizontally from center to side and back to center.

When Daniel tried to teach me how to swim, he took me to the public pool. He yelled at me to tread water with my arms. He told me to keep my legs still, or he would tie my legs together. The lifeguard asked us to leave. Daniel's father taught him how to swim in this way, but it wasn't in a public pool, it was in the Green River.

"He was drowned," acknowledged the police officer.

"The murderer is a good swimmer. He showed off to his school friends that he can swim using only his arms by tucking a shovel into his pant leg," I explained. "And he did this in the Green River." I'm hoping she will understand the picture.

"I got him," the police officer stated in a definite whisper.

"He showed off to his high school friends that he can swim using only his arms," Zeddy reiterated.

"No, he showed off to his college friends," I corrected her. I said "school friends", not "high school friends."

"I didn't think about it," Zeddy paused. "What was his college degree in?"

"Psychology", I replied.

"So, he learned how to fool people," Zeddy decided. She had a smirk on her face again.

"It is the same bachelor's degree as Ted Bundy," I reminded her.

"Ah," the crowd gasped. If it becomes a movie, everyone knows the serial killer's name.

"Why didn't his school friends suspect him of the murders?" Zeddy asked.

"They treated it as a joke. Even when one of the victims survived and reported that a man with a bristly blonde mustache raked brush over her and left her for dead, his friends just laughed and teased him about committing the murders. The victim's physical description didn't match the police suspect. So, the police assumed the victim had it wrong."

"Plus one for her, minus one for the police," Zeddy replied. She paused, tilted her head, and then accused, "You both killed him. You killed him together."

I didn't agree with her insult to the police, but I needed to address her allegation, "I don't do anything with him," I emphasized the word "anything". "I have a restraining order against him, a protection order," I corrected. I pause, "I don't have a copy, because he broke into my house and stole it." I asserted, "If he came anywhere near me, I'd call the police. Not that they've been that helpful." Generally, the police believed information from my ex-husband, even now that he was in prison.

I continued to explain, "Now in the state of Washington, the file has a message telling the reader not to use it. If anyone tries to add information to the file, there is a message to stop everything they are doing and come straight into the office."

"That is unlikely," Zeddy mocked. She refused to verify.

# April 11, 2024

My mother received a phone call. The police wanted to know where Lawrence was. The police said. "He had a traffic ticket, and he didn't show up for court. He missed jury duty. He has debts. There was now a warrant out for his arrest." The police file said to only share information with Lawrence's wife, and he's never had a wife. Was it real police calling? The caller gave my mother the impression Lawrence was on the lam.

It was after 9:00 p.m. on Bill's birthday. I pushed him in his wheelchair away from the theater. Pain radiated up his right side. The two-hour comedy show was a fun outing, but too long for his aching body. Laughter seemed to be an appropriate medicine for the occasion. Now Bill complained about the cold and the drizzle of rain. I slipped under an overhang to step out of the rain. I needed to scout the parking lot to make sure I had enough access to position the wheelchair before attempting the patient transfer into the backseat of my car. I learned to do this as a routine when I worked in West Seattle ambulating patients at a nursing home. My scouting mission was interrupted. A stranger stopped me as I attempted to walk away. The anonymous file she read instructed her to stop me as I tried to leave. I used my credit card to pay for the event tickets and my purchase was tracked.

"Are you the author of The Whiffle Ball Killer?" the stranger asked. She was oblivious to Bill's pain or his need to get back to nursing care.

"Yes," I answered, "That's me." I continued to monitor the weather for an opportunity to get my patient out of the cold and back to the nursing home.

"You don't have evidence of a murder," the woman accused. "Your ex-husband isn't in prison."

"You are looking up the wrong name," I explain.

"You haven't had any marriage in the last twenty years," she informed. She assumed the marriage would be recent and not one before my second marriage.

"The man in front of me is my second ex-husband. He isn't in prison," I said and patted his wheelchair handlebars. "There is no question about that." I put my hand out to show he was here in front of me. "You need to look up the name of my first ex-husband."

She looked down at Bill and then back up at me. "Why did you marry an old man?" she asked.

This was a thoughtless insult to say about a man on his birthday. "I didn't marry an old man," I explained. "I am older than he is." Social workers learn not to look up birthdates to avoid age discrimination. And then I'm forever explaining assumptions they make about my age. Why isn't it age discrimination to call someone an "old man" on his birthday? Her vocal tone wasn't kind or apologetic.

"You married Bill," she informed.

"I'm Bill," Bill interjected. He looked up at her and gave a nod.

So, she hadn't read my book. She had a different agenda. Two men walked up to us to join the conversation. "You can look up divorce decrees. Those decrees are court records and come up easier than marriage certificates which are county documents. Or you can look up my name changes. Each name change has associated paperwork. Or you could understand that I would know how many times I've been married," I explain. "Don't you think that makes sense?"

The woman didn't want to check. I don't know her name. I'll call her Zashia. "It would be a waste of time to check the database. There is no point in looking up the name. It's not in there, because you weren't married," Zashia explained. "You aren't old enough to be married to someone before. You would need your parents' permission as a minor," Zashia reasoned.

"I explained that my second ex-husband is younger than me," I reminded her. Why does she continue to assume that I needed parental permission? The local police don't believe I lived in Kent in 1984. They think my whole family would move for that to be true. They claim I'm too young to be married in 1984. The local police believe I wasn't born yet. The local police say the protection order in 1986 would be requested by my parents. My date of birth is on my driver's license. Why don't they check the date and calculate my age?

Zashia turned her attention back to me. "Do you know Ockham's razor?" she asked.

"Yes, I know Ockham's razor. 'The simplest solution is the correct solution,'" I quote. "It isn't about the most convenient solution. It is about the simplest solution, the one solution that fits all of the clues." It has become a common misconception about Ockham's razor to say that the one who made the report is the one who committed the murders. "The assumption of mental illness is the application that is the most complex solution, not the simplest and an incorrect use of Ockham's razor."

"She was married before," Bill defended. He followed the implications Zashia made. It isn't easy for me to follow the assumptions when I am addressing the allegations. I assume my responses are considered, instead of ignored. It makes it harder to understand the conversation.

"You don't have evidence he committed murder," Zashia accused.

"His DNA was a match for what was found on the victims," I said.

"The DNA could have been from a woman," Zashia responded.

"It was from semen samples," I informed her.

"Oh, I see," Zashia said sarcastically. In a mock statement, she added, "He was depositing his DNA on the victims after he killed them." The situation made no sense to her. "Why would a man murder someone and then intentionally leave incriminating evidence on the victim?"

"He wasn't just depositing the DNA," an attorney general inserted.

"There was post-mortem bruising," I explained. I was about to add post-mortem vaginal and rectal bruising, but she got the point. The expansion was unnecessary.

Finally, Zashia understood. Her eyes were in wide circles and her jaw dropped. For a moment she was speechless. At first, she was thinking of Jerry, a male victim. She hadn't considered what he did to women after he killed them.

"Man, you really have to spell things out for some people," the second attorney general said.

"She had it in her head that she was the bad one," the first attorney general explained to the second. Zashia assumed I was the bad one.

"My uncle Lawrence disappeared in the same year," I added. "Lawrence Otto Olsen," I clarified.

Zashia did a quick search in her database. She read, "Lawrence Otto Olsen: He was sticking up for a neighbor who didn't have a permit."

"Except that she did have a permit," I answered. "There were two copies of the permit in the file. One copy from when the permit was issued. And a second copy from when the permit was given to the contractors," I clarified. "They were reputable contractors. They obtained a copy of the permit and then," I explained and paused, "they did what they always do. They taped the permit to the front door." I took an angry exhale through my nose. "Daniel must have taken the permit off the front door. Then he called it in. He knew they didn't have the permit because it was in his hands."

"It was a prank," the first attorney general acknowledged.

"He wasn't sticking up for a neighbor who didn't have a permit," the second attorney general said. "He was sticking up for someone who did have a permit." He paused for emphasis, "It shows a different character trait." Lawrence wasn't trying to justify someone breaking the law. He was standing up for someone following the law who was wronged. The summary in the database was character defamation. The statement was used as a basis for "extenuating circumstances" that advanced his misdemeanor to be treated as a felony and the situation and took him into police custody.

"I wonder why the prosecuting attorney didn't pick up on that," Zashia said. She added about Lawrence, "The whole time he didn't know he was harboring the one who took the permit." She read the file, "He used the alias 'Ole.'" She asked, "Was that because of a criminal background?"

"Olsen, spelled S E N, is a Danish name," I explained. "It means the oldest son. As the oldest son of the family, he has the right to go by 'Ole Olsen' and he has claimed that right." I added, "It is a Danish tradition."

How could they think Lawrence has a criminal history? How did this bias start and what effect did it have?

Zashia smiled with an idea, "I'll ask them if they have seen Lawrence or anyone else going in or out of his house." She said, "I can do this in a way that doesn't cause alarm."

The first attorney general objected, "Your ability to do anything in a way that doesn't cause alarm is in question." He continued, "And this may be a murder case. That hasn't been taken into consideration."

The second attorney general noted the change of jurisdiction. Zashia worked on both sides of the river in either state. "I thought you were good at finding that information on Lawrence so quickly," he said and frowned. "But you aren't local." He was offended, "You are from Oregon." He said in an accusatory tone, "You stepped in because you didn't think we were doing our job."

"A social worker in Oregon said Kulik may need to be charged," I said. "There were two social workers that showed up at my work," I complained. "And they broke in and stole a brass trophy from 1954."

The second attorney general was furious and started to yell. I can't remember his phrase exactly. From what I remember it included profanity. The 1954 trophy was not checked in as police evidence in the murder case.

"Kulik has been charged. She's still fighting it," the first attorney general said after checking the database. He looked me in the eye, "That's where the problem comes in."

Ms. Kulik attempted to discredit my witness testimony. She was the same attorney who went after Albright while defending Washington state Governor Mike Lowry. Albright was an intelligent political campaign manager. Kulik portrayed Albright as mentally incompetent. Most people don't know that Albright sued and won $70,000.

Another case one year before mine played a role. Kulik defended CWU Professor Prigge who informed a mother about a college student's pregnancy and abortion. The family was strictly Catholic and held anti-abortion beliefs. Needless to say, this caused emotional trauma for the Catholic student.

Kulik made it a policy for her office to only communicate with the mother. This was to the extent that the mother would be contacted for the student's witness testimony instead of the student. The policy was read in our college classes.

The Catholic student won settlement money but signed paperwork not to use her college degree. I refused the buyout and refused to sign. I was successfully employed as a teacher before I attended CWU, and the state attorney general's office verified that there were no issues with my employment.

"I thought we were keeping her from using her degree," the one who stole the 1954 brass trophy said. "That is what I was told." She made the comment to Kalvin and Nerissa at Amazon. The only positive part of that conversation is that she studied the Green River Killer and verified the death of the man who left to buy groceries with a woman who appeared to be his girlfriend. She said, "Gary Ridgway said he didn't know anything about it."

I nodded, "The woman wasn't the girlfriend of the married man, just the first girl Daniel spotted. He had a way of defaming people, even after death."

I made no false complaints. I discussed a different man than the one they assumed. The names were repeatedly switched, and Daniel Bondehagen had a hand in that. He tainted the witnesses long before Ms. Kulik came onto the scene. And he encouraged my parents not to mention that I was married. He said, "I don't want to be implicated.".

The same Professor Prigge thought I grew up in the poor inner city. She incorrectly interpreted my accent. I never met someone from the poor inner city. Her assumption contributed to the personality profile in the anonymous file the FBI flagged. When people hear the word "gold-digger," they assume the "gold-digger" is a woman, not a man. This confusion allowed Daniel to continue his fraud without suspicion. People who read the file assumed I was advancing my socio-economic status, instead of marrying someone from a poorer background.

The second attorney general said to me, "But you do have a body don't you?" He was referring to the body found in 1984.

I thought he was referring to the skeleton found recently. "Yes, but I don't think that body belongs to either Jerry or Lawrence." I added, "I'm not sure who the body belongs to." Zashia looked at me in disbelief. She was frowning, quizzically. Her eyes were scanning up and down my face. Her mouth was gaping open.

The first attorney general said to the second attorney general, "I think you opened up another can of worms."

Zashia moved to write in the file. She noted, "Some of the entries were deleted."

"Hey," the first attorney general said. "Does that file allow you to make entries?" Zashia nodded. "Then write this," he looked over her shoulder and told her what to jot down.

It was troubling. "The body was dug up by the neighbor with his backhoe." I clarified, "He dug the body up with his backhoe accidentally."

The second attorney general responded in a consoling manner, "Backhoes have a tendency to do that."

The first attorney general said to the second attorney general, "Yep, you opened another can of worms. Now we need to find that backhoe."

I walked off to get Bill back to the nursing home. The passenger car door was blocked by a van. I had them wait until I transferred my patient.

[In April 2024, they were reading a file from 2021.] From what I overheard at a distance while loading the wheelchair into my trunk:

Their conversation continued. "He drove Lawrence's truck to the parking lot," the attorney general said. The Amazon warehouse parking lot is where Daniel was captured and that's how he arrived at this remote location at 6:00 in the morning in the snow, without public transportation. Lawrence's truck was found abandoned there.

"There is no other way Lawrence's truck could show up there," Zashia said. "There is no other way."

The attorney general continued, "Lawrence lost his appeal because his truck was seen driven around town." Lawrence was accused of driving with a suspended driver's license. Driving twice on a suspended license is prosecuted as a class four felony.

"That's just sinister," Zashia responded. "The only reason he was stopped was because of 'swatting'." She stopped to calculate, "That's too long to be in custody. He would be released to someone. I don't think he is alive."

At her comment I pause. I need to write down all possibilities of what happened. I blame myself if Lawrence was murdered. I tried to protect myself and my family. That is why I obtained the protection order. But Lawrence didn't take my protection order against Daniel seriously.

The song sparrows are chirping outside, gathering scattered birdseed off the ground. I mow the lawn and pull up weeds. It is something I can accomplish. I hope Lawrence is alive. If he is alive, writing this all down will help.

# The Approach

I refused to be swayed by the speculation of Lawrence's death. I checked the records. Lawrence remained the owner of his four-bedroom house. His house had a strong estimated value. The house had a lien of $15,200. This is a small amount to owe on a large house with a double lot.

Other people were living at Lawrence's house. I could not understand why. The caller told my mother the house was no longer owned by Lawrence. But the records clearly showed that it was not sold. The state can take possession of abandoned property after five years. But Lawrence can't be presumed dead unless he is missing for seven years. The timelines suggest that the property goes into the hands of the state first.

Lawrence wasn't driving his vehicle, so he didn't commit a traffic offense. If his personal driver got a ticket by camera enforcement, the driver couldn't be distinguished from Lawrence, unless he was pulled over. If Lawrence was pulled over, he would be in custody. If he is in custody, the police wouldn't be looking for him.

The pictures of Lawrence's house showed a garage door open. Why is the garage door not closing? What is piled in the garage? Why is the roof in disrepair? The front door is open. Who is leaving the front door open? Why? There is a ladder outside near the front door. A truck parked in front has a flat tire. It looks like packages were dropped off at the door and not taken inside. The lawn is mowed, but not watered. Who lives there now?

I'm not afraid of finding Lawrence. Or the mess that might be there. Or the current occupants pulling a gun on me. Or opposition from the police. I'm afraid of finding thick plastic folded with military corners. I'm afraid of finding seafoam green. I'm afraid of finding the things that seem harmless which point to someone more dangerous.

Back in 2001, as I prepared for a moving sale, I found an army cot in my garage. I didn't know what it was. My neighbor set it out for customers to see. It was a quick sale.

I found a Hawaii beach towel, black with pink flowers, in the garage. I called Bill's cousin to ask if it was his.

Bill's cousin asked, "Where did you find it? Was there anything else you found?" Then he said, "I think you had a visitor."

"No, there was no visitor," I answered.

Later that day a potential customer came to my house and said, "A man took down your garage sale signs and told people not to come. He said you sold items that weren't yours. He said he was a man who lived at your house."

"There are no men who live here," I explained to the customer.

"I'm just passing on what he said," the customer said as she was leaving.

Daniel was living in my garage and sleeping on the army cot. If he was living in garages and garden sheds, was he also Lawrence's periodic house guest needing a place to stay? Was that the reason Lawrence disappeared? Did Daniel drift to avoid detection by the police?

## Swatting Incident in 2017

I had a swatting incident in 2017. It was early morning and barely dawn. The sun was below the horizon. I was going on a walk up the ridge. I was wearing my black cotton jogging suit. I stopped at the intersection to cross the street. A man in a large truck is at the intersection. His headlights are off. I wait for him to pass before I cross. It was a good thing I saw him. Headlights don't turn off for at least another hour. He must have forgotten them this morning. He pauses. I can't figure out why.

He looks forward as if looking towards where he plans to drive. But his truck doesn't move. Finally, he takes a left turn and pulls into the daycare. He doesn't use his left blinker. No headlights, no blinker. He steps out of the truck and rushes up to the daycare door. He is an old man, tall, and thin, with a slightly hunched upper back and long legs. His face is thin. In his profile, his nose makes a triangle. His jacket is padded. His arms are down, but curve at his side while he walks, instead of staying close to his body, as if finishing a breaststroke. He bends his head down as he stands in the doorway. He knocks on the door. A polite woman answers the front door and lets him in. He looks up at her and smiles as he steps inside. He tilts his head back up as he greets her. She closes the door.

I continued my walk up the ridge. Then I cross the street to walk down the other side back towards home. A police officer stops me at the peak. He tells me he received a telephone call, "You match the description of a woman. Are you new in the area? Why are you wearing a black jogging outfit? Why are you out walking so early?"

The questions are confusing. Does the police officer think I am casing? I counted three other people out walking or jogging this early, including the woman who cleans the public buses. I explain, "I walk up the ridge and then jog on my way back down as a reward for making it to the top." I explain, "I'm not new to the area. I've lived here since 2006. I am a homeowner. I've been a homeowner since 2009. The daycare is in a rental house. I know their landlord. I know the family who used to live there."

"A man saw you as he was dropping off his kids," the police officer continued. "He said when he saw you all kinds of alarms went off. You were standing in front of the daycare."

"I was waiting to cross the street," I explained. "The intersection is there. The renters are so new, they didn't notice that there is an intersection." I'm thinking, "What kids? He didn't have any kids with him. There were no passengers that I could see. If he had alarms going off in his head, why would he leave the children alone in his truck? If he was concerned, why didn't he approach me instead of calling the police?"

"It might be some other reason," the police officer said.

I paused, "And one other thing. The truck driver had his headlights off." I decided, "Maybe he forgot to turn them on."

"Or maybe it was deliberate," the police officer said. "When he approached the street, he turned them off."

"What did the truck look like? What was the color?"

"It was so dark, I couldn't tell what color it was," I explained. "It was black as far as I know. But it may have been any dark color that looks black. It was raised up." I moved my hands up to show him. The wheel rim was smaller than the size of the wheels. I tried to draw a diagram in the air. And the truck was raised up for wheels of the wrong size."

"I'll find it," the police officer said. He continued on his way.

Later I saw the daycare owner outside. She recognized my jogging suit. I was upset at her for calling the police. "I wasn't expecting to see someone out here so early," she explained. She advised me to go for a walk later in the day.

"No, I've been in this neighborhood longer. I'm a homeowner. You are renting," I said. "You can get used to me taking a walk in the morning. Besides I counted three other people out talking a walk or jog."

"He said he was a grandfather of children at the daycare. But we didn't find who they were," she said. She was thinking, and her voice trailed off. "I don't even know his name. When he called the police, he gave them my name." He called the police on me without giving his name! "I think he is someone who knows you," the daycare owner decided.

# Early January 2021

After New Year's Day, I was walking to the post office and the neighbor stopped me.

"We are trying to figure out who the truck belongs to," the neighbor looked concerned. "It's not here today." He glanced over to the side of the road where the truck was usually parked. Each day a truck was parked on Main in front of the rental house.

The nights were long and the days short. When I turned the corner, leaving for work, I had to swerve to miss the truck parked along the road. It wasn't that it was parked too close to the corner. The truck was legally parked. The truck just stood out wider than I expected. I learned to roll the passenger window down to see where the truck was to avoid hitting it on my way out. The dark night obscured the truck. I don't even know what the color was. All I noticed was the galvanized steel toolbox container in the truck bed. "It isn't mine," I responded without concern.

Twice I had the opportunity to identify Lawrence's truck, the incident at the daycare and the truck parked along Main that I swerved to miss.

# The Ordeal

I went to the last place Lawrence was seen. The garage door remained open. The roof over the garage was rotted. Moss was thick on the roof. Debris was piled in the driveway. The debris was worse in the garage and blocked the garage door from closing. Several truckloads would be needed to clear the debris. The littered items looked heavy.

Yet, care was given to the house. The front door was closed. The packages on the front step were gone. The ladder was put away. The lawn was mowed. Cherry tomatoes grew in raised beds in the front yard.

Sitting in the driveway, next to the debris, there was a short man with a bushy yellowish-white beard. His beard was so thick it was impossible to tell where his mustache stopped, and his beard began. His lips were invisible under all the thick facial hair. His nose was slightly flushed. He sat on a cooler drinking a cold beer. I approached the man with a thick beard and introduced myself.

"Hi, I'm Gary," he said. This was Gary Maupin. From the information I received from my mother, she assumed he was a mythical character, yet Mr. Maupin was real.

Maupin explained Lawrence's plight. "Lawrence took in a couple of people who betrayed him. They were robbing him blind. After that, he didn't know who to trust." He set his bottom jaw firm, "I told him, you've known me for ten years. You can trust me."

"Have you seen Lawrence recently?" I asked.

"Yes, I saw him this morning," Mr. Maupin replied. This was the best news I've heard in a long time. He pointed up the road, "Lawrence is at the courthouse now over the sidewalk."

I looked down at the ground and only saw gravel. I was confused. There was no sidewalk. I was led to the backyard. Mr. Maupin explained "The city has plans to put in a sidewalk at the other end of Lawrence's lot. Lawrence went down to city hall to file paperwork for the judge to fight the new sidewalk. He is willing to speak up, where the other neighbors won't."

"Are they reimbursing him for that land?" I asked.

"No," Mr. Maupin said.

Well-groomed flower bushes lined the edge of the property. "This is a double lot, isn't it? Would a sidewalk make it harder to sell the other lot?" I asked.

Mr. Maupin stopped to think, "Yes, I suppose it is a double lot."

"You could put a one bedroom or two bedroom house there," I commented.

"How big would it be?" Mr. Maupin asked.

"One thousand square feet," I said. "A two bedroom house with one thousand square feet." Mr. Maupin smiled.

I looked across the yard. "Is that the smoker?" I asked.

"It's the whole pig smoker," Mr. Maupin nodded in confirmation. "It is designed to hook up a truck and be hauled behind." He wasn't fond of it. "I spent too many hours preparing the pig. I started at 10:00 at night and worked all through the next day. By the time I was done, I was so sick of it, I couldn't eat any of the pig."

"It was tender though," I praised with a smile.

On the way back I noticed the break in the kitchen window. The duct tape that covered the break had peeled off. There was no second pane to shield the air. Wood was stacked too close to the house. Mr. Maupin showed me the thick metal post that held up the roof in the southwest corner. He patted it with his right hand. Lawrence paid $5,000 for a permit to install it.

The garage roof was collapsed. There was a hole in the roof four feet across. Green foliage grew on the tarp as if it was always meant to be there. Supplies to repair the roof lay in the driveway and had been eaten away by rodents. I asked, "Are there any holes in the roof inside the house?"

Mr. Maupin mentioned something about an elevator shaft. I thought this referred to Lawrence's elevator business. But no, Mr. Maupin clarified, "There is a hole in the roof inside the house, this eroded the floor. It is like an elevator shaft all the way to the basement." Mr. Maupin explained, "Lawrence paid for a new roof, and he was taken. Lawrence thinks the man will do it, but he's on his deathbed now. There is no chance." He shook his head.

The beautiful house I remembered was very different now. The construction company swindled him. Each time Lawrence sees that hole, it must remind him of betrayal. The golf course-like green lawn was changed too. Yet the weeds were pulled, and the vegetable garden and flowers were taken care of.

"Habitat for Humanity took a look at it," Mr. Maupin continued. "They built that house next door. They offered to rebuild this one too, but Lawrence turned them down. He's stubborn. Where does he get that from?" Those were opportunities that only came around once.

It would be like Daniel to take the permit off the front door and report the owner for not having one. It's a prank he would do. He would rob someone blind too. Giving him a place to stay made no difference.

When Daniel dated Joan, the girl whose hair was as red as a flame, she gave him a place to stay. But he repaid that generosity by stealing from her and then taking her life when she wanted out.

Lawrence's house would have been the nicest place Daniel had to stay, compared to a garage, garden shed, or crawl space. He couldn't avoid pranking or stealing from a generous host. While Daniel lived as a homeless person, he convinced my parents he was a good investor.

Mr. Maupin explained that Lawrence was held in jail for 30 days after the issue with the missing permit and DUI charge. He was told that if he confessed, he would be released. Otherwise, he'd stay another 30 days. He was released on house arrest and found guilty of a felony. A multimillionaire, a good neighbor, generous to a fault treated as a felon and chained to the dining room table.

Lawrence was written out of his parents' Will, along with me. What was the reason for the family spat between Lawrence and his sister?

## Wolf Unclothed

Daniel expected to have me committed to a mental institution and then take control of my finances and assets. He needed to show that I was mentally ill, not getting along with family members, unable to keep a job, and dangerous. Without the "dangerous" stipulation, his plan would not be successful. I didn't know how he planned to pull this off.

At a Society of Women Engineers luncheon, a couple of the ladies in my group left the table to use the restroom. When each returned, I was interrogated. The first one to return did not believe the attorney who represented the state governor would now face charges from the FBI. Although this is the checks and balances part of our government.

I was quizzed when the next friend returned to the table. "Someone wants to keep me from telling my story," I said.

"Your sister sure does," she replied.

"That doesn't make sense," I said. "The Attorney General's Office tasked my sister with looking out for this. I think someone is using the file the FBI flagged."

My friend agreed, "Oh, right."

A few tables down I heard a woman's voice, "Did you check your information? She's just having lunch with her friends, and you didn't check your information?" A man with brown hair went from entranced in my conversation to a startled expression.

The clues were vague and hard to decipher. One clue was, "It would make a lot of sense if your ex-husband had a girlfriend who is a psychologist." Another clue, "We refer to any family member as your mother, as a generic phrase."

Rita was the sister they referred to. She isn't my sister, but my father's sister. She is the psychologist mentioned in the file. And she is a Catholic who believes, "There is nothing more important than your marriage."

Rita received money "off the top" of my inheritance. This was the infusion of money. With her cut, the investment would never have a positive return, even if Daniel was a real investor.

My parents thought Daniel seemed to have it together. And they assumed he was a solid investment for their money. My parents expected I would leave with Daniel in the same way the prodigal son left his father. I didn't ask for an early inheritance. Daniel asked for my inheritance early. I never saw a penny of it.

"I thought she would feel cared for," my mother explained to the relatives. Daniel is in custody for murder, but they believe it is a mistake.

"He was a serial killer," Lawrence's brother said. "But more than that. He was a thief," with emphasis as if a thief is worse. He noticed my facial expression. "I just mean in addition." He looked at my parents, his mouth dropped open and he said, "They gave him all of that money after they found out he laced the wedding cake with bread mold." He said, "He violated his Anti-harassment Order, and they want her to visit him in prison."

Mr. Maupin gave me Lawrence's new contact information. I invited Lawrence to our family reunion. There might be someone there he didn't want to see. I respected his hesitancy, after everything he went through.

But who continued to spread stories about Lawrence? Daniel was arrested in 2021. Rita wasn't a likely suspect. The swatting seemed to continue. In my case, it was from the use of an anonymous file the FBI flagged. Was there a similar file on Lawrence? Why did Zashia think Ole was an alias to mask a criminal record? Or was there another player?

What part did my father play? The Washington Attorney General had a conversation with the family back in September 2022.

My father complained to the attorney general. "He's going to tell me I'm not doing enough to control her."

"Are you frightened of him?" I asked.

"I never thought about it," my father confessed.

"You didn't give him all that money because you knew he was safe," my mother said. "You knew he was dangerous. You were going to hand your daughter over to him knowing he was dangerous."

My father admitted he gave Daniel the locker key along with the gate access code. It was Daniel who stole my rare coins.

My father had my mother give Daniel $200 each month for decades. My mother gave Daniel enough money to take me on an Alaskan cruise. When he did contact me, he only asked to go out to dinner, and he requested to go Dutch.

My father sold his new tractor to give Daniel the money. He sold my mother's acreage and gave Daniel money. And my father bought a timeshare at the beach and allowed Daniel to stay there.

My mother couldn't make payments on her credit card without the money going to a different account that she couldn't access. The money would be posted to her account. Then the payment information would be missing, and the money transferred to an account without her name. She was charged with a late fee, even though she made a large payment.

I called the credit card company and demanded they give her a new account number and refund the unauthorized transaction. Daniel knew my mother needed to make a payment. The reversal left Daniel with an over-the-limit credit card balance and late fees.

My father was moaning in fear, "He wasn't supposed to get into trouble. He'll yell at me. I don't know what he is going to do when he yells at me."

The attorney general nodded, soaking this all in, "Usually the girl who is abducted needs retraining. This time it is her parents who need retraining." My father was both obedient towards and frightened of my ex-husband. He wanted to bail Daniel out of jail. The attorney general assured him, "No judge would accept your money."

# The Capture

Once Daniel Bondehagen asked me, "How do you think Jesus did this?" He showed me The Gospel of Luke 4:28-30, "When they heard this, all in the synagogue were filled with wrath. And they rose up and put him out of the city and led him to the brow of the hill on which their city was built, that they might throw him down headlong. But passing through the midst of them he went away." I showed him another Bible passage. He shook his head, "I'm more interested in this."

It was Passover when Jesus passed through the crowd. The people had a singular focus. Purity. No one wanted to shed blood. If they shed blood or came into contact with a dead person, they would not be allowed to join in the feast. They couldn't make it look like an accident. There were too many people there. Jesus wasn't invisible. The people simply let Jesus pass.

Judas waited until the feast was complete to lead the soldiers to Jesus. Two years later Herod waited until the feast was complete to lay hands on Peter. A Jew who was exposed to a dead body needed to wait seven days and miss the festival. This practice was to the extent that the dead remained unburied until the feast was over.

I've never written before about Daniel's capture.

A man in the crowd to my left ducked behind some of the workers standing in the drop-off area of the parking lot. He attempted to pass through the crowd in the same way Jesus had. He knew my peripheral vision wasn't as good in my left eye. He planned to stalk me from the beginning.

I thought, "If I am being stalked, I won't be able to catch him." This feeling of hopelessness didn't help.

The anonymous file read, "If she looks like she doesn't know what you are talking about, she is just being coy." During those questions people were told to ask me, Daniel stood by listening for the answer.

"He could be in this parking lot right now. What would you do?" Zaria asked at the front door as I attempted to exit. She was instructed to wait until I started to leave and then stop me. She mocked. She didn't care if she was frightening me. Zaria scanned the parking lot with her eyes.

Zaria's question didn't turn my head. But a familiar laugh from the parking lot did, a clown laugh. I quickly turned my head. It was too late. I only caught a glimpse of him, a profile of a man walking, or maybe it was nothing. Maybe nothing was turning and walking behind a man who was standing and watching their conversation. I decided to watch "The Nothing." Profiles are harder to identify. All I caught was a profile of a man or maybe it was just my imagination. My mind might be playing tricks. I followed him with my eyes to the location I thought he had gone.

Then I abruptly returned to my conversation with Zaria who was standing at the door, who was demanding an answer to her question. It was now or never. I played the aces in my hand. I never let anyone know what I knew. I let it out.

The Amazon worker in the parking lot who was standing and watching felt my eyes pass through him. He knew I wasn't looking at him. I didn't focus on him. He knew I was turning to look at someone passing behind him, from his left side to his right. He heard the crunch of footsteps on the decorative gray rocks. He followed the natural direction and speed of my head and eyes and turned in the rhythm of my glance. He turned his head to the right to look over his shoulder at the man behind him. A man who looked like an aging Tom Petty was lurking in the parking lot. A young woman standing a few feet to the right, turned her body to the left to take a look behind. The nothing now had a face. Daniel was no longer invisible in the crowd. And they weren't going to let him pass.

Three people further back in the parking lot came up from behind him to block his exit. They were hemming him in. They weren't hemming in my imagination. Daniel was there. He was standing, lurking, for no reason when he should have been many miles away. That was enough. The young woman asked if she should call the police. More people came up from behind to stop his exit, five, and then eight. The Amazon workers were ready to hold him until the police arrived. They refused to move. Security came to intervene. The police searched for All Points Bulletin (APBs) and found a few for murder. The Federal Marshall was contacted, and they secured jurisdiction. Daniel was held first on suspicion of murder and then held indefinitely.

"He thought you'd never report him," the state attorney general said.

Viola, Daniel's mother, covered for him without question. Viola covered for Daniel when Thomas thought Daniel ran a red light. With his parents, he had no punishment. Daniel expected the same from the Green River Killer. Whoever was caught first would take the fall for all the murders. Daniel expected the same from me. The lack of accountability was the cause for his actions. This same lack of consequences became his vulnerability.

The Amazon night shift manager asked me not to tell where Daniel was captured. He wanted to avoid a panic in the building. The manager did such a good job keeping the information under control, the information wasn't passed down from the night shift to the day shift. "I don't see why they need it," he said. It was to the extent that the day shift assumed there was no murderer.

A man listening in said, "You expect this with a murder case and look for it. The only thing that makes this strange is people are continuing after he is in prison." Daniel intentionally created confusion through swatting. The confusion helped him escape murder charges and helped him continue fraud schemes. With continued confusion, Daniel was able to harass from behind bars.

Later Zashia said, "I suspected she was the mastermind behind it. Now I see that is wrong." In a taped phone conversation: "You didn't tell us these things were illegal," Zashia said to her former professor.

"You're recording this, and you didn't tell me?" the professor of social work asked.

"You told us we didn't need to," Zashia reminded him. "This is my plea bargain and I'm taking it."

There would be no plea bargain for Daniel. "What's the difference between you and John Gacy?" his psychiatrist asked.

[John Gacy is Patches the Clown.]

"I never got caught!" Daniel boasted.

"Well, I'm going to return you to your cell now," the psychiatrist replied.

Daniel waited for the jubilee year, the fiftieth year on the day of atonement. He thought in the jubilee year his sins, murders, post office fraud, bank fraud, credit card fraud, thefts, break-ins, pranks, and financial debts would be absolved. He believed that God was required to forgive his sins and give him a clean slate. God had no choice. He believed he had power over God.

Even the crimes Daniel was certain he got away with, came back to haunt him. The authorities told me there was an incident near the border that summer solstice night in June 1984. One of the campers was murdered. The man I thought was a ranger, was the man at the campsite who roared in anger. It wasn't a bear that roared.

Daniel killed a man for no other reason than his location was convenient. Yet, the murder wasn't entirely random. It was planned.

As I recall the events in a new light, I realize my camping companion couldn't go one week without committing murder. And that week was our honeymoon.

Daniel was charged as an accomplice to the murders at Meeker Street Bridge. He was the one who buried the bodies. In a way, Daniel was the real River Man. He tucked the shovel into his long thermal underwear and swam the river. He was found guilty on eight charges of murder, and that number is increasing. He has more verified kills than any other man in American history.

Daniel robbed Lawrence blind and divided the family. This helped him with his con as an investor. These financial schemes produced his other unsuspecting victims, riches to rags.

During the jubilee year, slaves were allowed to return to their families. The original owners had their possessions returned. Debts were absolved. But the atonement was never intended as an abuse of God's grace.

The jubilee year was a call to return home. And that is just what I intended to do. I plan to reconcile with Lawrence when he feels ready to trust. In small steps, through God's grace, after my family receives "retraining after abduction," we can work toward healing.

www.ingramcontent.com/pod-product-compliance
Lightning Source LLC
Chambersburg PA
CBHW070617030426
42337CB00020B/3837